DOLL ALDERTON

Biography

Reflections on Love and Growing Up

Melissa Anne Cruz

TABLE OF CONTENTS

CHAPTER 1

BOYS

CHAPTER 2

A HELLRAISER HEADS TO LEAMINGTON SPA

CHAPTER 3

BEING A BIT FAT, BEING A BIT THIN

CHAPTER 4

GOOSEBERRY FOOL: MY LIFE AS A THIRD WHEEL

CHAPTER 5

BEING BJÖRN AGAIN

CHAPTER 6

THE UNCOOL GIRLS OF UNCOOL CAMDEN

CHAPTER 7

'NOTHING WILL CHANGE'

CHAPTER 8

TOTTENHAM COURT ROAD AND ORDERING SHIT OFF AMAZON

CHAPTER 9

MY THERAPIST SAYS

CHAPTER 10

HEARTBREAK HOTEL

CHAPTER 11

I GOT GURUED

CHAPTER 12

ENOUGH

CHAPTER 13

HOMECOMING

CHAPTER 1

BOYS

For some, the happy shrieks of their siblings playing in the garden defined their adolescence. Others heard the chain rattle of their beloved bike as it hobbled down hills and valleys. Some will recall hearing birdsong on their way to school, or hearing laughter and footballs being kicked in the playground. It was the sound of AOL dial-up internet for me. I can recall it now, note for note. The tinny first phone beeps, the reedy, half-finished squiggles of sound that indicated a half-connection, the high one note that indicated some progress, followed by two abrasive low thumps, some white fuzz. The silence then suggested that you had made it through the worst of it. 'Welcome to AOL,' murmured a calming voice, the 'O' inflected upward. Then it says, 'You have an email.' To make the torturous time pass faster, I would dance around the room to the sound of the AOL dial-up. I made a routine consisting of ballet moves: a plié on the beeps, a pas de chat on the thumps. When I got home from school, I did it every night. Because that was my life's music. Because I spent my adolescence on the web. A little background: I grew up in the suburbs. That's all there is to it; that's the explanation. My parents made the horrible decision to relocate us out of a basement flat in Islington and into a larger property in Stanmore, the last stop on the Jubilee line and on the extreme outskirts of North London, when I was eight years old. It was the city's blank margin; an observer of the pleasure rather than a partygoer. Growing up in Stanmore is neither urban nor country. I was too far away from London to be one of those cool kids that went to the Ministry of Sound and dropped their 'g's while wearing nice vintage clothes from a surprisingly good Oxfam in Peckham Rye. But I was too far away from the Chilterns to be one of those ruddy-cheeked, savage, rural youths who wore old fisherman's jumpers and learned to drive their father's Citroen when they were thirteen, and went on walks and took acid in the woods with their relatives. The North London suburbs were an identity vacuum. It was as beige as the luxurious carpets that decorated every room in the house. There was no art, culture, historic structures, parks, or independent stores or restaurants. There were golf courses, Prezzo locations, private schools, driveways, roundabouts, retail parks, and glass-roofed shopping malls. The women all looked the same, the houses all looked the same, and the automobiles all looked the same. The only way to express oneself was to spend money on homogenised assets such as conservatories, kitchen expansions, automobiles with built-in satnav, and all-inclusive holidays to Majorca. There was nothing to do unless you wanted to play golf, have your hair highlighted, or go shopping at a Volkswagen dealership. This was especially true if you were an adolescent dependent on your mother's availability to transport you in the aforementioned Volkswagen Golf GTI. Farly, my best friend, was only a three-and-a-half-mile bike ride away from my cul-de-sac. Farly was and still is unlike anyone else in my life. When we were eleven years old, we met at school. She was and still is the polar opposite of me. She is black, whereas I am light. She is a little short, and I am a little tall. She plans and schedules everything, whereas I wait until the last minute. She prefers order, but I prefer chaos. She loves rules; I despise them. She has no ego; I believe my piece of morning toast is important enough to justify broadcasting on three social media channels. She is always present and focused on the task at hand, whereas I am always half in life and half in a fanciful version of it in my imagination. But we make it work. Nothing in my life has been more fortunate than the day Farly sat next to me in a maths lecture in 1999.

The routine with Farly was always the same: we'd sit in front of the television, eating mountains of bagels and crisps (though only when our parents were away - another characteristic of the suburban middle classes is that they are particularly precious about sofas and always have a strictly no eating' living room) and watching American teen sitcoms on Nickelodeon. When we were done with Sister, Sister, Two of a Kind and Sabrina the Teenage Witch, we'd go to the music channels, staring slack-jawed at the TV screen while scrolling between MTV, MTV Base, and VH1 every ten seconds, hoping for a specific Usher video. When we got tired of that, we'd switch back to Nickelodeon + 1 and watch all of the episodes of the American adolescent comedy we'd seen an hour before on repeat. Morrissey once described his adolescent years as "waiting for a bus that never came," a sense that is only heightened when you reach adulthood in a setting that resembles an all-beige waiting room. I was bored, miserable, and lonely, wishing away the hours of my childhood. Then, like a brave hero in shining armour, AOL dial-up internet appeared on my family's enormous desktop computer. Then there was MSN Instant Messenger. It was like pounding on the wall of a prison cell and hearing someone tap back when I downloaded MSN Messenger and started adding email address connections - friends from school, friends of friends, friends in other schools I'd never met. It was like discovering grass blades on Mars. It was like turning on the radio and hearing the crackle smooth into a real voice. It was an escape from my suburban drudgery and into a plethora of human life. MSN was more than just a tool for me to communicate with my pals as a teenager; it was a destination. That's how I remember it: a room I sat in for hours on end every evening and weekend, until my eyes went bloodshot from gazing at the computer. Even when we moved out of the suburbs and my parents generously sent my brother and me to France for vacations, it was still the room I occupied every day. When we arrived at a new B&B, the first thing I did was ask if they had a computer with internet - usually an ancient desktop in a dark basement - and I would unashamedly sit chatting on it for hours while a moody French teenager sat behind me in an armchair waiting for his turn. Outside, where the rest of my family sat by the pool and read, the Provençal sun beat down, but my parents understood there was no debating with me when it came to MSN Messenger. It served as the focal point for all of my friendships. It was my personal space. It was the only thing I could truly call myself. As I already stated, it was a location. My first email address was munchkin_1_4@hotmail.com, which I created in my school's IT room when I was twelve years old. I chose the number 14 because I figured I'd only be emailing for two years before it became childish; I gave myself enough time to enjoy this new fad and its different idiosyncrasies before the address became obsolete on my fourteenth birthday. I didn't start using MSN Messenger until I was fourteen, and during that time I tried willyoungisyum@hotmail.com to convey my newfound love for Pop Idol's 2002 champion. After giving a barnstorming performance as Mister Snow in the school's production of Carousel, I also attempted on thespian_me@hotmail.com. When I acquired MSN Instant Messenger and liked the overflowing MSN Messenger contacts book of school buddies I had accumulated since the address's genesis, I resurrected munchkin_1_4. But, maybe most importantly, guys were introduced. I didn't know any boys at the time. I hadn't spent any time with a boy in my entire life, save from my brother, small cousin, dad, and one or two of my dad's cricketing buddies. MSN, on the other hand, brought the email addresses and avatars of these new floating Phantom lads; these were kindly donated by various girls at my school - the ones who would hang out with lads on the weekends and then graciously pass their email addresses across the student population. These guys were famous on MSN; every female in my school would add them as a contact, and we'd all have our fifteen minutes of fame talking to them. The boys' origins might be divided into three categories. The first was a girl's mother's godson or a family member on the periphery of her life with whom she had grown up. He was a year or two older than us, tall and lanky, with a deep voice. Someone's schoolboy neighbour was also included in this group. The cousins or second cousins of someone were the next classification. Finally, and most exotically, a boy whom someone had met while on a family vacation. This was the Holy Grail, because he might be anywhere, as far away is Bromley or Maidenhead, and you'd be talking to him on MSN Messenger as if he were in the same room. What lunacy; what adventure. I rapidly compiled a Rolodex of these wayward boys, labelling them with the word 'BOYS' in my contacts list. Weeks would pass while we talked about GCSE choices, favourite music, how much we smoked and drank, and 'how far' we'd 'been' with the opposite sex (always a ominously laboured piece of fiction). Of course, we had no idea what someone looked like; this was before camera phones or social media profiles, so all you had to go on was their little MSN profile photo and their description of themselves. I'd go to the trouble of using my mother's scanner to upload an image of me looking great at a family meal or on vacation, then painstakingly crop out my aunt or grandpa using Paint's crop tool, but it was usually too much trouble.

The introduction of virtual lads into the realm of our schoolmates brought with it a new set of disputes and drama. There would be constant speculation about who was speaking with whom. Girls would profess their love for boys they'd never met by entering the boy's first name into their username, with stars, hearts, and underscores on either side. Some girls thought they were having an intimate online conversation with a boy, but these usernames would tell a different story. Sometimes, girls from neighbouring schools who you'd never met before would add you to ask if you were chatting to the same boy they were. You might occasionally accidentally expose an MSN relationship with a boy by writing a message to him in the wrong window and sending it to a buddy instead, and this would always go down as a cautionary story in the common room. Tragic degrees of tragedy would ensue. MSN had a complicated etiquette; if both you and a boy you liked were logged on, but he wasn't talking to you, a failsafe way to get his attention would be to log off then log back on, as he would be notified of your re-entry and reminded of your presence, hopefully resulting in a conversation. There was also the option of concealing your online status if you wanted to avoid chatting to anyone other than one specific contact. It was a complicated Edwardian courtship dance, and I was a thrilled and ready player. These lengthy correspondences rarely ended in a physical meeting, and when they did, it was almost always a heartbreaking disappointment. Farly decided to meet Max with the double-barrelled surname, an infamous MSN Casanova known for delivering girls Baby G watches in the mail, at a newsagent in Bushey one Saturday afternoon after months of conversing online. She arrived, took one glance at him, and fled behind a trash can for cover. She watched him call her phone number from a phone box over and over again, but she couldn't face the reality of a face-to-face meeting and ran back home. They continued to talk on MSN for hours every night. I had two of them. The first was a catastrophic blind date that lasted less than fifteen minutes in a shopping mall. The second was a boy from a local boarding school with whom I'd talked for over a year before our first date at Pizza Express in Stanmore. We had an on-and-off connection for the next year, mostly because he was always locked up at school. But every now and then, I'd go to see him, wearing lipstick and carrying a handbag full of packets of cigarettes I'd bought for him, like Bob Hope being sent out to entertain the troops during WWII. He didn't have internet access in his dorm, so MSN was out, but we made up for it with weekly letters and long phone talks that made my father age with sorrow when he received a three-figure monthly landline phone bill. When I was fifteen, I had a love affair with Lauren, a wild-haired girl with freckles and kohl-rimmed hazel eyes, that was more all-consuming than anything that had ever happened in the

windows of MSN Instant Messenger. We'd seen one another at the odd Hollywood Bowl birthday party since we were youngsters, but we finally met properly over dinner in one of Stanmore's many Italian chain restaurants through our common friend Jess. The link reminded me of everything I'd seen in each romantic film I'd ever seen on ITV2. We chatted till our jaws were dry, we finished one other's sentences, we made tables turn around as we laughed like drains; Jess went home, and we sat on a bench in the bitter cold after being thrown out of the restaurant just to keep talking. She was a guitarist searching for a singer to form a band; I'd sung at a sparsely attended open-mic night in Hoxton and wanted a guitarist. The next day, we started rehearsing bossa nova renditions of Dead Kennedys songs in her mother's shed, with the initial draft of our band name being "Raging Pankhurst." We then modified it to 'Sophie Can't Fly,' which was even more perplexing. Our first job was in a Turkish restaurant in Pinner, with only one customer who wasn't a member of our family or a school buddy. We moved on to do all the major names: a theatre foyer in Rickmansworth, a pub garden's decrepit outbuilding in Mill Hill, and a cricket pavilion just outside of Cheltenham. We busked on any street without a cop present. We sang at the reception of any bar mitzvah that would have us. We also had a passion for the innovative way of multi-platforming our MSN content. We found early in our acquaintance that, since the invention of Instant Messenger, we had both been copying and pasting discussions with boys onto a Microsoft Word document, printing them off, and storing the pages in a ring-binder folder to read before bed like an erotic novel. We imagined ourselves as a two-person Bloomsbury Group of early 2000s MSN Messenger. But, just as I was developing a friendship with Lauren, I left suburbia to attend a co-ed boarding school 75 miles north of Stanmore. MSN could no longer satisfy my curiosity about the opposite sex; I needed to know what they were like in real life. The ever-fading smell of Ralph Lauren Polo Blue on a love letter no longer satisfied me, nor did the pings and drumming of fresh messages on MSN. I went to boarding school to try to adjust to boys.
(Aside: and thank God I did. Fairly remained on for sixth form at our all-girls school, and when she arrived at university, having never spent any time around boys, she was like an uncut bull in a china shop. On the first night of freshers' week, there was a 'traffic light

party,' where singles were urged to dress green and couples were encouraged to wear red. Most of us assumed this meant a green T-shirt, but Fairly appeared at our halls of residence bar wearing green tights, green shoes, a green dress, and a large green bow in her hair, accompanied with a mist of green hairspray. She might as well have had I WENT TO AN ALL-GIRLS SCHOOL tattooed across her brow. I will be eternally grateful that I had two years on the nursery slopes of mixed contact at boarding school; otherwise, I worry I might have fallen foul of the can of green hairspray come freshers' week.)

As it turned out, I had nothing in common with most boys and little interest in them until I wanted to kiss them. And no male I wanted to kiss wanted to kiss me, so I might as well have stayed in Stanmore and continued to enjoy a series of dream relationships played out in the fertile plains of my mind. I blame my high expectations for love on two factors: the first is that I am the kid of parents who are almost shamefully in love with each other, and the second is the films I watched in my early years. As a child, I had an unusual love for old musicals, and having grown up totally hooked on Gene Kelly and Rock Hudson films, I had always expected boys to carry themselves with the same elegance and charm. However, co-ed education quickly dispelled this perception. Consider my first political lesson. I was one of just two girls in a class of twelve and had never sat with so many boys in one room in my life. The best-looking lad, who I had already been told was a known heartthrob (his older brother, who had departed the year before, was dubbed 'Zeus'), passed a piece of paper to me down the table as our teacher described what Proportional Representation was. The message was rolled up with a heart painted on the front, leading me to imagine it was a love letter; I opened it with a sly smile. When I unfolded it, however, there was an image of a creature, helpfully annotated to notify me that it was an orc from Lord of the Rings, with 'YOU LOOK LIKE THIS' scribbled underneath it.

Farly came to see me on weekends and marvelled at the hundreds of guys of different shapes and sizes strolling the streets, sports bags and hockey sticks slung over their shoulders. She couldn't believe my good fortune in being able to sit in rows next to them in the chapel every morning. However, I found the reality of boys to be a little disappointing. Not as hilarious as the girls I'd met there, not as interesting or kind. And, for some reason, I could never totally relax with any of them. I had ceased using MSN Messenger religiously by the time I graduated from high school. My first term at Exeter University came to an end, and with it, the arrival of Facebook. Facebook was an internet treasure trove for boys - and this time, even better, you have all of their crucial information compiled on one page. I would constantly scroll through my uni friends' images and add anyone who caught my eye; this would swiftly escalate into conversations back and forth and planned meet-ups at one of the several Vodka Shark club nights or foam parties that week. I was at a campus university in a cathedral city in Devon; we had no trouble finding one other. If MSN was a blank canvas on which I could paint colourful dreams, Facebook messaging was merely a meet-up tool. It was how students selected their next triumph; it was how they planned their next Thursday night.

By the time I graduated from university and returned to London, I had firmly abandoned my habit of cold-calling potential love interests on Facebook with the zeal of an Avon representative, but a new pattern was emerging. I'd meet a man through a friend, at a party, or on a night out, acquire his name and number, and then build an epistolary relationship with him via text or email for weeks and weeks before confirming a second in-person meet-up. Perhaps it was because this was the only way I'd learned to get to know someone, with enough space between us for me to curate and filter the best version of myself possible - all the good jokes, all the best sentences, all the songs I knew he'd like, usually sent to me by Lauren. In exchange, I'd send her tunes by email to her pen buddy. She once remarked that we sent good new music to each other at wholesale prices, then passed it on to love interests with an "emotional mark-up."

This type of correspondence almost invariably resulted in disappointment. I gradually realised that it's preferable for those first dates to take place in person rather than in writing, because otherwise the gap between who you envision the other person to be and who they actually are grows larger and wider. Many times, I'd manufacture a person in my imagination and create our chemistry as if I were writing a script, only to be crushed when we met again in real life. It was as if, when things didn't go as planned, I'd thought he'd be handed a copy of the screenplay I'd prepared, and I'd be irritated that his agent had apparently forgotten to provide it to him to memorise.

Any woman who spent her early years surrounded solely by other girls will tell you the same thing: you never get over the notion that boys are the most interesting, alluring, repugnant, weird creatures to roam the world, as deadly and legendary as a Sasquatch. Most of the time, it also means you're a lifelong fantasist. And how could you not be? For years, all I did was sit on walls with Farly, kicking bricks with my thick rubber soles and staring up at the sky, trying to think of something to keep us distracted from the endless sight of hundreds of females wandering about us in similar uniforms. When you attend an all-girls school, your imagination gets the everyday training of an Olympic athlete. It's incredible how accustomed you become to the tremendous fire of fantasy when you retreat to it so frequently.

I always assumed that my fascination and fixation with the opposite sex would fade after I graduated from high school and began my adult life, but little did I know that I would be just as naive about how to interact with them in my late twenties as I was when I first signed on to MSN Messenger.

Boys were an issue. It would take me fifteen years to repair.

CHAPTER 2
A HELLRAISER HEADS TO LEAMINGTON SPA

I was ten years old the first time I got drunk. I attended Natasha Bratt's bat mitzvah with four other lucky chosen girls from our class. The wine was flowing and the smoked salmon was circling in their Mill Hill back garden's sun-flooded marquee; the women's hair was blow-dried into aggressively undulating trajectories, their lips a uniform frosted beige. And for reasons I'll never understand, the catering staff served glass after glass of champagne to all of us girls, who were clearly prepubescent in our Tammy Girl strapless dresses and butterfly clips in our hair. At first, it felt like a wave of warmth was washing over me, my blood racing and my skin buzzing. Then, as if all the screws in all my joints had been freed, I was as springy and light as freshly baked dough. Then there was chatting: amusing stories, theatrical impressions of instructors and parents, harsh jokes, and the greatest swear words. (This three-step pattern is still how I feel early drunkenness to this day.)

The father-daughter dance to Van Morrison's 'Brown Eyed Girl' was cut short when one of the girls, who was slightly further along than the rest of us, threw herself belly-first on the dance floor and wiggled manically underneath the legs of both parties, like a flapping fish out of water. I swiftly followed suit before we were both removed and reprimanded by an irate uncle. However, the night had only just begun. I decided it was time for my first kiss, followed by my second (his closest buddy), and finally by my third (the first's brother). Everyone got involved, swapping and testing out kissing partners as if they were desserts at a table. This suburban child orgy was eventually disbanded, and we were all taken to the front room and served black coffee; the door was locked, and our parents were summoned to pick us up. We were reprimanded a second time by our headmistress on Monday for representing the school in a bad light' (this was frequently an accusation levelled at me during my scholastic years, and it always struck me as a slightly weak takedown, especially since I had never chosen to represent the school; rather, my parents had chosen the school to represent me).

I was never the same after that night, the contents of which filled the pages of my diaries well into my adolescence. I had developed a craving for booze at a way too young age. At any family gathering, I pleaded for small, diluted glasses of wine. At Christmas, I'd slurp the delicious, throat-catching liquid from the guts of liqueur chocolates, hoping for a hit. When I was fourteen, I figured out where my parents kept the key to their drinks cabinet and began drinking capfuls of cheap French brandy when they were gone, relishing the warm, dizzy cloud it cast over the burden of homework. Sometimes I'd drag Farly into my secret suburban bingeing - we'd guzzle their Beefeater gin and refill it with water, then sit cross-legged on the plush carpet and argue over the correct answer to Who Wants to Be a Millionaire?

I've never despised anything more than being a teenager. I was completely unsuited to the state of adolescence. I was desperate to be considered an adult, to be regarded seriously. I despised relying on others for anything. I'd rather have swept floors than been given pocket money, or walked three miles in the rain at night than have a parent give me a ride home. When I was fifteen, I was looking up the prices of one-bedroom flats in Camden so I could start saving with my babysitting money. At the same age, I was hosting 'dinner parties' with my mother's recipes and dining table, forcing my friends to come over for rosemary roast chicken tagliatelle and raspberry pavlovas with a Frank Sinatra soundtrack when all they wanted to do was eat burgers and go bowling. I desired my own set of friends, my own schedule, my own house, my own money, and my own life. Being a teenager was one big, irritating, mortifying, exposing, co-dependent disgrace that couldn't come soon enough for me. I believe that drinking was my modest act of independence. It was the only way I felt like an adult. All of my friends' drinking byproducts - snogging, shrieking, secret-swapping, smoking, and dancing - were enjoyable, but it was the relevant adultness of booze that I enjoyed the most. I would act out fictitious scenes from everyday adult life. I would boldly go into local off-licences and skim the backs of bottles while holding imaginary chats into my Nokia 3310 about 'a casual drinks party on Saturday' or 'a nightmare day in the workplace' or 'where I left the car'. In the four o'clock rush out of school on a Friday, I would place myself in the middle of the corridor within earshot of teachers and shout, 'WE'RE STILL ON FOR DINNER, YEAH?' at Farly, 'I FANCY A FULL-BODIED BOTTLE OF RED!' and enjoyed the slightly puzzled look on their faces as they passed

me. Well, screw you, I'd say. I'm doing something you're also doing. I'm drinking something. I'm a grown-up. Please take me seriously.
It wasn't until I was sixteen and went to boarding school that I really developed a taste for heavy liquor. My co-ed school was the last of the English boarding schools to have a sixth-former bar on campus. On Thursdays and Saturdays, hundreds of sixteen to eighteen-year-olds descended on a small basement, claimed their two cans of beer, and rubbed up against each other on a dark, hot dance floor to the sound of 'Beenie Man and Other Dance Hall Legends'. My boarding house was fortunately situated across the street from the bar, allowing for a quick stumble home at eleven o'clock, where our matron would put out boxes of pizza for us to drunkenly consume together. It also meant that our house garden was utilised as a hedonistic, after-hours playground, and my housemistress would strap a pit helmet to her head and walk out into the bushes fishing for semi-clothed, fumbling children half an hour after curfew. There was always a fantastic moment when we'd overhear her summoning the boy's housemaster from her study after sending any female caught in the garden up to bed with no pizza and sending the boy back to his house.
'I discovered your James behind my rhododendron shrub with my Emily with his pants down,' she'd remark in her thick Yorkshire brogue. 'I've dispatched him; he should be with you in ten minutes.'
Before we got to the bar, all of the teachers knew we drank. We'd smuggle bottles of vodka disguised in empty, washed-out shampoo bottles into our suitcases, and we had an endless supply of Marlboro Lights beneath our pillows. When I smoked a spliff and had bloodshot eyes, I'd wet my hair as if I'd just gotten out of the shower and blamed it on the shampoo. The unspoken rule was that we trusted you to know your boundaries, so don't be a jerk about it. Drink and smoke, but don't act inappropriately or make it obvious. Overall, the method worked. There was always the occasional kid who went too far and shattered a chair or attempted to hump a young maths instructor on duty, but the rest of us held it together. Teachers were generally quite respectful of the students; they regarded us as young adults rather than children. My boarding school years were the only ones I enjoyed during my teens. University would never be a perfect environment for someone who has an unhealthy relationship with alcohol, but my God, I chose the worst one imaginable the day I

filed a UCAS application to Exeter. Exeter has long been recognized as a university for half-soaked, semi-literate Hooray Henrys, nestled in the verdant, rolling hills of Devon. If you ever meet a middle-aged man who still plays lacrosse, knows every drinking game rule, and sings better Latin than English when he's drunk, he probably went to Exeter University, also known as 'The Green Welly Uni' in the 1980s. I only applied because Farly had done so. Farly just applied because it was good for Classics and she likes going to the beach. I only attended because I didn't get into the one course I really wanted at Bristol, and my parents insisted that I attend university. I am still sure that the three years I spent at Exeter made me dumber than when I arrived. I did very little work; I went from being a voracious bookworm to not reading a single page of a book that wasn't a set text (and I'm not even sure I finished one of those). From September 2006 until July 2009, I did nothing except drink and shag. Everyone only drank and shagged, pausing only briefly to eat a kebab, watch an episode of Eggheads, or shop for a 'Lashed of the Summer Wine' themed pub crawl. It was the most politically passive place I had ever visited, far from being the hotbed of radical thinking and impassioned activism I had hoped for. There were only two protests I was aware of during my entire time there: the first, a student-body stand against the removal of curly fries from the Student Union Pub's menu; and the second, a young woman's petition to have a bridleway built on campus so she could ride her pony to and from her lectures. I would be bitter about the years I squandered in Exeter if it hadn't been for the one thing that made the whole sad experience worthwhile: the women I met. Farly and I met a group of females who would become our closest friends within the first week. Lacey was a gobby and lovely golden-haired drama student; AJ was a dazzling brunette from a rigorous all-girls school who sang hymns when she got drunk; and Sabrina was the charming blonde, full of energy and wide-eyed enthusiasm. Sophie, a red-headed South London girl who was amusing and boyish, was frequently coming around to fix things in our flats. Then there was Hicks. Hicks was our ringleader, a Suffolk-born Stig of the Dump with a bleach-blonde bob, crazy eyes in a cloak of sparkly blue makeup, long, coltish, youthful legs, and tits I could spot in a crowd. I'd never encountered anyone like her; she was fearless and dangerous, astute and audacious. When you were with Hicks, nothing seemed to have an effect. It was as if she ran her own kingdom, with its own rules, where the night ended at one p.m. and the next night began the next afternoon, and where an old man you met at a pub would end up as a temporary lodger in your house. She was utterly there, incredibly gorgeous and enviably rock 'n' roll. Her impulsive, bottomless thirst for fun set the tone for the next three years. I frequently wonder if the aggressively laddish and macho culture at Exeter explains why we behaved the way we did as students; whether my all-female circle of friends was attempting to equal that intensity with our behaviour. It was a continuation of American frat-boy culture from the movies we grew up watching, intersected with the obnoxious hierarchical system of public education. We liked urinating in groups behind skips (Farley and I were once caught and admonished for doing this on the edges of a graveyard, naked bottoms on display for passing motorists, one of which happened to be a police car). We stole traffic cones that had accumulated in our living room. On club dance floors, we snatched each other up and hurled each other around. We discussed sex as if it were a team activity. We were full of bravado and rodomontade, and we worked with merciless honesty and zero rivalry with each other, frequently boring each other's perspective with meaningless long, intoxicated lectures about how amazing our friend was. We had a 'visitors' book' for 'overnight guests' to sign on their way out the next morning at the ramshackle house with the red door where I lived with AJ, Farly, and Lacey. In the back garden, there was a defunct 1980s television that sat there come rain or shine. Slugs that littered our hallway, which I'd saved one by one after a night out by taking them outside and depositing them on a particular patch of grass (Lacey later acknowledged they put pellets down for them but didn't tell me). It was a period of extreme, bizarre depravity. A world in which two of my friends stayed up all night dancing before going to Exeter cathedral for a Sunday service and warbling hymns while wearing gold Lycra; a world in which Farly once woke up for a nine a.m. lecture to find me and Hicks still downstairs drinking Baileys with a middle-aged cab driver we'd invited in the night before. We were the worst kind of pupils you could imagine. We were rash, self-absorbed, childish, and fiercely careless. We were Broken Britain, as we used to shout as we strolled to the pub. I now cross streets and get off tubes at a stop early to avoid being in the same vicinity as the loud, foolish, self-satisfied exhibitionists that we were. If I ever wanted to gauge the depth of the binge-drinking culture in my university group of friends, I only had to look at the people who came to visit. When my younger brother, Ben, came to visit for a few days when he was seventeen, he was 'appalled' by the half-clothed, barely conscious apparitions he encountered in the clubs I took him to, taking particular offence at a section of one bar dubbed 'Legend's Corner' because only members of the rugby team were permitted to sit there. He later told my parents that his three-day visit to Exeter was one of the key reasons he declined to go to university and instead chose to attend theatrical school. Lauren moved to Oxford to study English, and we did a university exchange program a few times. She'd take the Megabus down to Exeter for a few days with me, and I'd return to Oxford with her, wandering around the Magdalen deer park, imagining an alternate life in which I read books and wrote bi-weekly essays and lived in a spire-topped house with no television(s).

Lauren's first visit seemed like I was teaching her how to be a student. On a night out, I ordered a bottle of rosé from the bar for five pounds.

'All right,' she said. 'Is that for just the two of us?'

'No, that's just for me,' I said as Lauren looked around at my pals, each with their own bottle of wine and a single plastic glass from the bar. "We each get one.' She watched her first episode of America's Next Top Model the next day while lounging on the sofa eating pricey, sweet, doughy pizza. That afternoon, she ran across the lacrosse player who famously started writing his Human Geography dissertation in the pub at two p.m. on the day it was due. Lauren claimed she always felt comfortable and recharged when she returned to Oxford after a much-needed break from her rigorous undergraduate experience of intellectual peacocking. I always returned to Exeter feeling depressed and ready to leave after a few days in Oxford. When depicting the bubble of unanswered bad behaviour with no penalty that was my undergraduate experience, I frequently refer to an incident featuring Sophie - now a prominent and respected journalist covering critical LGBTQ and women's issues - to remember how far we've come. She laid by the water next to a pissing male buddy one night after leaving a Thai full moon party at a quayside club dressed as a Thai fisherman, believing she was going to vomit due to the eight-shot bucket of Vodka Shark she had just purchased and consumed. A half-comatose buddy of a friend was resting on her back like a starfish on her side. Sophie sensed an opportunity to both transport a young woman to safety and possibly strike gold. But after she arrived at the girl's dorms, she realised this wasn't going to happen, so she took another cab back to the club and ordered another bucket of Vodka Shark. She then met a boy who stated he was going to a late-night curry house for takeout. Sophie accompanied him, yelling 'PASANDA, PASANDA' as she banged on the shop counter. They placed their order, went to his house, and devoured a mound of curry. Sophie vomited into a perspex dish in the boy's bedroom and set it aside. She dozed out in his bed, awoke the next morning dressed as a fisherman, peered at the puke bowl but did nothing, and then got the boy's micro scooter and scooty all the way home.

'We were just trying to collect stories for each other,' she says now, when I wonder how we could have all had such an infantile desire for irresponsibility and so little self-awareness. 'That's what we exchanged. It wasn't to impress anyone but each other.'

It was clear that, while everyone enjoyed drinking, I particularly enjoyed drinking. I'd consume alcohol at racing speed. Much of it was because I like the flavour and sensation of alcohol, but I also drank as a student for the same reason I drank on my own when I was fourteen: putting alcohol into my brain was like pouring water into squash. Everything had been muted and mellowed. The sober girl was plagued by anxiety, sure that everyone she cared about would die, and concerned about what others thought of her. The inebriated teenager smoked a cigarette with her toes 'for fun' and cartwheeled on dance floors. I graduated from Exeter a month before my twenty-first birthday, and by September, I was studying for a Masters in Journalism in London. Believe it or not, this was the year that my partying peaked; I had been rejected unceremoniously and violently, and I poured myself into weight reduction to distract myself from my pain, and I drank and smoked for the distraction. I hadn't lost my taste for it yet. It was just as exhilarating at twenty-one as it had been eleven years before during Natasha Bratt's bat mitzvah. On one of many Saturday nights that year, I sat on the tube, staring out at the dazzling metropolis as I went from the suburbs to central London on the Metropolitan line, which rode like a cantering horse on the tracks. All of London is mine, I reasoned. Everything is feasible. This year, my hedonism came to a climax in a most un-rock 'n' roll way: a long ride in a taxi. In my defence, it was Hicks who started it. She became a household name among Exeter students in our third year when she left a night out at a bar on the High Street, hopped into a taxi, and requested the driver to take her to Brighton. She spent every money she had on transportation and remained on the floor of a hotel suite with her married pals on a romantic holiday. The next week, she returned to Exeter to tell her story. The night started when my new curly-haired brilliant buddy from my Journalism MA degree, Helen, and I went to our friend Moya's place for a glass of wine and to speak about our upcoming big exam. Helen and I drank bottle after bottle of wine in the sun, becoming boiling drunk before leaving Moya's around midnight. I decided that the night wasn't done and that I wanted to go out, so we boarded a bus from West Hampstead to Oxford Circus. However, I became noticeably drunker the moment the bus journey began - which also took an absurdly long time due to a traffic accident - so at some point while in transit I convinced myself that we weren't on a bus to Oxford Circus, but rather on a coach to Oxford city centre. Helen, who spoke similarly to me, agreed with my persuasive hypothesis. Lauren had graduated from Oxford at this point, so I didn't call her; instead, I texted a few of her acquaintances I'd met on my visits there and knew were in their final year. The texts were hardly understandable, but they said something like, 'Me and my friend Helen had accidentally gotten on a coach to Oxford. We're almost there - where should we go for a night out, and would you care to join us?'

We got off near the main Topshop, which was bigger than I recalled it being the last time I visited Oxford. We stood outside the shop as I called everyone I'd ever met at Oxford University, still unable to believe I was in London. Helen and I agreed that the night out was a bust, but it was too late for me to catch the final tube back to my parents' suburban home. So we took another bus back to Helen's Finsbury Park flat, which she shared with her boyfriend, and she invited me to sleep on their sofa. Refusing to let go of my intoxicated fantasy, I assumed that we were in Oxford University Halls, and that a friend of Helen's was still a student here. Helen went to bed, and I checked my phonebook to see if anyone I knew was available for a

party. I called my friend Will, a tall, wild, wiry Canadian with long curling hair and opal-blue eyes. I'd always had a huge crush on him.
'Hello, dear,' he said, his voice garbled from the booze.
'I want a party,' I declared.
'Come on, then.'
'Where are you?' I inquired. 'Are you still in university in Birmingham?'
'Warwick. 'I live in Leamington Spa,' he explained. 'I'll text you the address,' she says.
I walked out of Helen's apartment and went in search of a taxi company. I located a modest, wooden-fronted minicab firm after ten minutes of wandering the streets, the alcohol slowly leaving my system as I finally realised I was in London and not Oxford. I stated that I needed a car to transport me to Leamington Spa and that money was not an issue - except that it had to be £100 or less because that was all I had in my account and I was at the limit of my overdraft. One of the three amused men walked behind the glass barrier to retrieve a dusty map of England from his drawer. To the amusement of his colleagues, he unfurled the map and theatrically stretched it across two pushed-together tables. They all clustered around it as one plotted the voyage with red pen dashes, as if he were the captain of a ship organising an attack on pirates. Even in my intoxicated state, I thought it was a little much. '£250,' he finally said.
'That's RIDICULOUS,' I exclaimed, my pearl-clutching, middle-class customer-rights fury palpable, as if he were the one making the most ridiculous request of the two of us.
'Lady, would you like to go to three counties away at three o'clock in the morning? £250 is an extremely acceptable price.'
I talked him down to £200. Will agreed to pay the remaining £100.
I began sobering up on the M1 at four a.m. (that's a sentence I hope none of the rest of you ever have to utter or write down in the rest of your lives). But it was too late to turn back - that's how I often felt in the thick of these late-night exploits, convincing myself that I was simply getting my money's worth out of my youth. A Margaret Atwood quote hung from the ceiling like a lampshade during this time in my life. When you're in the middle of a story, it's just a blur; a black roaring, blindness, a wreckage of smashed glass and splintered wood; like a house in a whirlwind, or a boat crushed by icebergs or pushed over the rapids, with everyone on board

powerless to stop it. It's only after that that it begins to resemble a story. When you are telling it to yourself or to another person. It would pay off in the end, I reasoned as I peered out the window of my car on the highway, the sky turning to dawn. The anecdotal mileage in this will be endless. I came at half past five o'clock in the morning. Will met me at the entrance and handed me five twenty-pound notes. I was ecstatic that I had made it there. The voyage and the destination where the story; what happened next was practically unimportant. We stayed up all night drinking, talking, and lying in bed half-clothed smoking pot and listening to Smiths albums, only pausing briefly for some half-assed snogging. At eleven a.m., we fell asleep. I awoke at three p.m. with a bad headache and a terrible feeling that the punchline to the joke wasn't as humorous as I had believed the night before. My bank account was empty. I grabbed my phone, and there were dozens of worrying messages from pals. I'd forgotten I'd emailed Farly a photo of myself joyously smiling in the back of the cab at four a.m. while flying down the highway with the message: 'QUICK TRIP TO THE WEST MIDLANDS!!'

I devised a strategy. My teenage boyfriend, with whom I had maintained a hazy friendship, was studying medicine at Warwick University. I could remain with him for a few days until some overdue money from my weekend work as a promo girl arrived, then catch a train home in time for my Journalism MA exam on Tuesday. But when I texted him, he said he was on vacation. Sophie called when my phone rang.

'Is it true you're in Leamington Spa?' she said when I answered the phone.

'Yes.'

'Why?'

'Because I wanted an after-party and my friend Will, who lives in Leamington Spa, was holding one.' Will, who was still half asleep, offered a guilty-as-charged thumbs-up.

'OK, that doesn't make sense,' she admitted. 'How are you getting home?'

'I'm not sure. I was planning on staying with an old boyfriend, but he isn't here, and I don't have any money for the train.' After a long silence, I could hear Sophie's worry for me turn to frustration.

'All well, then I'll book you a bus home,' she responded. 'Does your phone have a charge?'

'Yes.'

'I'll email you the specifics as soon as it's finished.'

'Thank you, thank you, thank you,' I expressed my gratitude. 'I'll repay you.'

Sophie booked me a seat on the longest coach route she could locate, reasoning that I needed some alone time with my thoughts to reflect on the repercussions of my actions. I found up on a coach with a rowdy London-bound hen party, much to her chagrin. On the way, we all drank tequila shots and they gave me a sombrero to wear. When I called Sophie the next day to thank her for rescuing the day, I inquired if she was unhappy with me.

'I'm not annoyed with you, Dolly, I'm worried for you,' she explained.

'Why?' I inquired.

'Because you were so inebriated that you assumed you were in Oxford city centre while you were standing outside the Oxford Circus Topshop. Do you realise how vulnerable that makes you? 'Are you really that intoxicated and wandering around London?'

'I'm sorry,' I responded angrily. 'I was just having a good time.'

'How many of our friends have to go bankrupt taking cabs throughout the UK before this madness stops?'

(A few months later, it would only take one more - Farly - from South West London to Exeter. She was in a cab on her way home from a club when she received a text from a boy she liked who was still at university, and she asked the driver if he could turn around and take her to Devon instead. To this day, she shrugs off accusations of excess and maintains the entire journey cost '£90 and a package of fags'. The figure has gradually increased in value as we have pressed her on it.)

But what mattered was that they were all good stories. It was the driving force behind my early twenties. I was a six-foot human metal detector for fragments of possible anecdotes, crawling through existence with my nose pushed to the grass in the hopes of finding anything to dig at. Another night, Hicks and I went to a swanky London hotel because she had assured it was a hub for 'bored billionaires with buckets of booze who desire the company of fun, young people'. We did, indeed, come across two middle-aged men from Dubai who ran a curry house on Edgware Road and one of those English Language 'universities' over a mobile phone shop on

Tottenham Court Road. Hicks and I went through our regular ritual of telling the well-rehearsed made-up story of how we met on a vacation. I was singing with the band, her husband had thrown himself overboard, and we'd started talking one day while sitting alone on the upper deck, smoking and staring out at sea. They invited us to their friend Rodney's house, where they told us that he was a "party boy" - the ubiquitous euphemism for "generous with his alcohol and drugs." We all hopped into their waiting car, and their driver drove us to a tower block on Edgware Road that was far from the Studio 54 promise of excess and grandeur. Hicks and I strolled together to the door, and in the lift, I texted Farly the address of where we were in case anything happened to me that night, a morbid ritual she had grown accustomed to. The door was opened by a Cypriot man in his mid-seventies wearing stripy pyjamas.

'My God!' he exclaimed as he examined us. 'It is too late!' In despair, he threw his hands in the air. 'I'm too old for you!'

Our two new pals assured us that the celebration would be brief and that we only wanted a few beers. Rodney welcomed us in and asked what we wanted to drink. He said cocktails were his specialty, motioning to his well-stocked 1970s liquor cabinet. I requested a dry Martini. Rodney captivated me, especially the dozens of framed images of grandchildren that were strewn across every available surface. We went about with our Martinis, him still in his pyjamas, and he told me all of their names, ages, and character descriptions. Meanwhile, Hicks was doing what she always did on nights like this: she was philosophising with one of the Dubai millionaires, gesticulating dramatically while monologuing about French existentialists, her eyes popping out of her head like forget-me-nots from cracks in the pavement.

Rodney and I sat on his sofa, and he told me about his prior mythology: failed business attempts, the bar he ran that was now a Waitrose, and the models who shattered his heart. At one point, he interrupted his story, folding up a five-pound note for the coke he had set up on his coffee table, and leaned back to stare at me.

'You know, it's weird, you remind me of a woman I met a couple times in the 1970s. She has long blonde hair and eyes like yours. For a while, she was dating a friend of mine.'

'Oh yeah?' I said, lighting a cigarette. 'Who exactly was she?'

'Barby. 'I believe her name was Barby.' I swallowed, recalling a story my mother told me about a fun-but-awful nickname she was given in her early twenties.
'Barbara,' I said. 'Barbara Levey,' she says.
'Yes!' he exclaimed. 'Do you know who she is?'
'That's my mother,' I said. I envisioned her in bed in the suburbs, wondering what she'd think of her daughter getting high with a 75-year-old Cypriot man she'd met in the 1970s. I went into the next room, interrupted Hicks' one-woman literary salon with her infatuated and indifferent audience, and told her we had to leave right away. She promised a fantastic 'after-party' at the curry house one of the men owned on Edgware Road. I informed her that we had already arrived at the after-party. I wondered if I had somehow ended up in the murky hinterland of after-parties and was now stuck there all the time. I was wondering if I needed a ladder.
But I can't say everything was tragic because it wasn't. My companions and I were convinced that what we were doing was a fantastic act of empowerment and independence. My mother often told me that this was a foolish attempt at feminism, because imitating the most obnoxious male behaviour was not a sign of equality ('She was so harmful to the cause, that Zo Ball,' she once said). But I still believe that my years of partying were a defiant, joyous, and powerful act; a refusal to utilise my body in the way that was expected of me. Many of the recollections revolve around me and one of the girls leaving a scenario we were bored with or didn't enjoy, just to spend time with one other. I was ravenous for adventure, and I quenched my hunger with other ramblers. And it instilled in us a gang mentality that we have never broken.
Some of my memories are happy, while others are painful, and that was the reality. Sometimes I danced till dawn in a circle of my best friends, and other times I collapsed on the street while sprinting for the night bus in the rain and lay on the damp pavement for far too long. Sometimes I walked into a lamppost and ended up with a purple chin for days. But every now and then, I'd wake up in a loving tangle of hung-over girls, full of nothing but comfort and love. I now see folks from those slightly fuzzy years who claim to have spent an evening with me drinking in the corner of a house party, and I panic because I can't remember it. I cringed with shame a year or so ago when a black cab driver asked if my name was 'Donny' since he was

very sure he'd picked me up in 'a great state' wandering down a London street with no shoes on in 2009.

But a lot of it was wonderful, carefree enjoyment. Much of it was an expedition, through cities, counties, stories, and people, accompanied by a gang of adventurers in neon tights and too much black eyeliner.

And, at the very least, I thought I had finally demonstrated to everyone that I was an adult. At the very least, I was finally taken seriously.

CHAPTER 3
BEING A BIT FAT, BEING A BIT THIN

'Do you still love me?' I inquired.
'No,' he replied. 'No, I don't think I still love you.'
'Do you like me at all?' I inquired. There was a pause.
'I don't believe so.'
I hung up the phone.
(I've since told individuals that if they're dumped, they should lie about it. The 'falling out of love' crap is awful. The 'I don't fancy you' material is fantastic.)
I was twenty-one years old and had recently graduated from university. And my first proper boyfriend had just called to break up with me. Despite being absolutely and utterly unsuited for one other, Harry and I had been dating for a little over a year. He was a sports fanatic who did a hundred press-ups before bed every night, was the social secretary of the Exeter University Lacrosse Club, and wore a T-shirt with the words 'Lash Gordon' on the front. He despised overt shows of emotion, tall ladies wearing heels, and being overly loud. So, basically, everything that constituted my personality at the moment. He believed I was a flop, and I thought he was a jerk.
Our whole relationship was spent arguing, not to mention the fact that we never spent any time apart. In our final year of university, he basically lived in the flat I shared with Lacey, AJ, and Farly, and he had moved into my parents' house for the summer while doing an internship.
One of our lowest points came at the conclusion of that long, hot, nervous August, when we boarded a train to Oxford for Lacey's twenty-first birthday party. After the main course, I wandered away from my seat and came across a swimming pool that looked interesting. So I stripped naked and went for a swim, and when a few pals came seeking for me, I pushed everyone else to do the same. The night devolved into a massive pool party, and I took on the role of a nude poolside Master of Ceremonies. Harry went insane. The next morning, Farly and AJ hid behind a tree with uncontrollable laughter as they watched him yell at me, 'YOU WILL NEVER SHOW UP LIKE THAT AGAIN!' My head-hanging shame was

heightened by the fact that the pool had been over chlorinated and my bleached hair had turned a vibrant bottle green.

We didn't have much in common. But he wanted to be my first proper boyfriend, which was a good enough excuse to go out with someone when I was nineteen.

I was staying with a friend in an East London flat the night he called, avoiding the long trip from Stanmore by starting my journalism course. Farly arrived an hour later at one a.m., having driven from her mother's house, and informed me that she was driving me home.

On the way back, I was inconsolable, attempting to recall our chat to Fairly but remembering very little of it. He called when my phone rang. I informed her that I couldn't speak to him. She pulled over, took up the phone, and placed it to her ear.

'Harry, what have you done?' she demanded. On the other end of the call, I couldn't understand what he was saying. 'Fine, but why do it to her over the phone? Why couldn't you come see her and do it in person?' She barked once more. On his side, there was more muddled conversation. Farly was attentive. 'YEAH? 'WELL, FUCK YOU,' she said, hanging up and tossing her phone onto the seat behind her.

'What exactly did he say?'

'Really, nothing,' she said.

That night, Farly slept in my bed. And then there was the night after that. She stayed for a fortnight, and I didn't return to the flat. It was my first heartbreak, and I had no idea the overriding feeling would be such severe bewilderment; as if I had no reason to trust anyone ever again. I had no understanding what had happened or why it had happened. I only knew I hadn't done well enough. I couldn't eat either. I'd heard about the aftereffects of a breakup before, but I never dreamed it would affect me. I was and had always been a very hungry girl. Perhaps the most hungry of them. I'd never managed to stick to a diet for more than two days. My entire family enjoyed meals, as did Farly and I. My mother, a natural cook who grew up with Italian grandparents, began teaching me to cook when I was five years old, placing me on a chair next to her so I could help knead dough or whisk eggs at the kitchen counter. Throughout my adolescence, I cooked for myself, and at university, I prepared for everyone. When I was six, my first diary entry was an enthusiastic record of what I had eaten that day. The crispy baked potatoes on coastal holidays in Devon, the colourful, sticky jam tarts of my tenth birthday, the roast chicken of every Sunday night, bathing the dread of the school week in gravy, recalled phases of my life. No matter how bad life got, no matter how excruciating the suffering, I was always certain I'd have room for seconds. I was never considered overweight, but my body type was frequently referred to as 'a large girl'. I came from a long line of big giants. My brother, God bless him, was a six-foot-seven youngster who had to shop in stores like 'Magnus' and 'High and Mighty'. I was five foot ten by the time I was fourteen. I was six feet tall by the time I was sixteen. But I wasn't one of those adorable tall, lanky adolescent half-foal, half-human girls - I had large shoulders and hips. I was the polar opposite of the girls photographed in the pages of Bliss and portrayed in the book series The Baby-Sitters Club. My physical being was not well-suited to being a teenager, just as I was not psychologically built for it. As a teenager, I found it difficult to be so tall since I never understood how much I was supposed to weigh because every female was half my height and talked about their 'fat weight' as being a weight I hadn't been since childhood, which caused me immense humiliation. This, combined with boredom eating and puppy fat, resulted in my shopping for size 16s when I wasn't yet sixteen. I was aware that I was larger than my peers and that I was occasionally labelled as obese, but I had trust that my body would make more sense when I wasn't a child. My parents' extremely drunk and spectacularly overweight friend Tilly grabbed my love handles like she was steering a ship at a barbecue when I was fifteen, declaring to the garden that 'is chunky girls have got to stick together' and telling me in no uncertain terms that men like a bit of meat on a girl', before I received a conspiratorial wink from her husband, who was, incidentally, also the width of a Vauxhal. When I went to boarding school, I gradually lost weight, and by the time I came to university, I was a comfortable size 14 - but I didn't mind that I wasn't really slender. I continued to kiss the boys I desired to kiss. I could dress in Topshop. I also enjoyed cooking and eating. That was the trade-off, I realised. Nonetheless, here I was. Finally, I couldn't eat anything. I was filled with a sickly yellow feeling from head to toe, and my appetite - my most dazzling asset - had fled. My guts were twitching. My throat was constantly clogged. Mum would offer me bowls of soup in the evening, assuring me it was simple to swallow, but I'd only eat a few spoonfuls and throw the rest away when she wasn't around.I stepped on the scales after a fortnight. I had dropped a stone. I stood naked in front of the mirror for the first time in my life and saw the very beginnings of what I had been trained to believe were the actual characteristics of femininity. Waist, hip bones, collarbones, and shoulder blades are all smaller. I felt a flash of something finally making sense in this new environment that I didn't comprehend, where the boy I'd lived a house and life with for over a year was suddenly horrified by me. Because I had stopped eating, my body was altering. It was successful. In the midst of the chaos, I discovered a basic formula of which I was the master. Here was something I could manage, something that would take me somewhere fresh, somewhere I could be someone else. In my reflection, I found the answer: stop eating.

I made a project out of my new objective; I weighed myself every day, calculated my steps and calories, did sit-ups in my bedroom every morning and night, and took weekly measurements. I survived solely on Diet Coke and carrot sticks. I'd retire to bed or take a hot bath if I wanted to eat something. More weight was removed. I lost it pound after pound, and it never seemed to stop. This provided me with energy that served as a substitute for meals at first; I felt like a high-speed train that was magically running on empty. Another month has passed, and another stone has fallen. My period did not arrive, which both scared and encouraged me. At the very least, it signified that something was changing both inside and outside of me; at the very least, I was getting closer to becoming someone new. I was hunkered down at home at this time, when I wasn't at lectures. I was still hurting from the breakup, and I didn't want to socialise. Alex, Harry's sister, who I had been very close to during our relationship and who, happily, stood by me through our break-up, was the first to detect something was wrong. We were skyping every day because she had recently moved to New York. I stood up in the middle of one of our conversations one day, and she saw my entire body for the first time in months.

'Where are your tits?' she said, widening her eyes as she examined me up and down, leaning into her camera.

'They're present.'

'No, they aren't. Your stomach is also like an ironing board. 'What happened, dolls?'

'Nothing, I've merely lost some weight,' she says.

'Oh my darling,' she frowned. 'Are you still not eating?'
Others were less astute. I started going out more and seeing university pals. People expressed their condolences for Harry's death. People informed me that he had a new girlfriend. People complimented me on how great I looked over and over. Every compliment was like a meal to me. I went out and drank constantly to distract myself from the agony of hunger. My mother, becoming increasingly concerned, would put plates of food on the kitchen table for me when I returned home from a night out. She correctly assumed that I would be more likely to eat then. When I arrived home, I learned to go directly to bed. I'd lost three stone by December. In three months, I lost three stone. I found it more difficult to summon the ideas and tight routines that had stopped me from eating up until that moment. I was fatigued, my hair was thinning, and I was continuously, bone-chillingly cold. I sat in the shower to attempt to warm up, but the water was so hot that it burned my back and left marks. I lied to my frightened parents about how much I'd eaten that day and when I planned to eat next. I'd have dreams about eating mountains and mountains of food and waking up in tears because I'd mistakenly shattered the spell I'd set. Hicks stayed at Exeter after the rest of us graduated for an extra year. Sophie, Farly, and I planned to drive down one weekend to spend the weekend with her and visit all of our old haunts. It also meant I could see Harry, who was in his final year there, which I hoped would feel like a full circle and bring me some closure. I told him we needed to give each other our belongings back, and he agreed to meet with me.
On a Saturday evening, the girls drove me to his house and parked outside.
'MATE, WE'LL WAIT RIGHT HERE,' Hicks yelled out the car window, her feet and a cigarette dangling from it. I approached Harry's front door and rang the doorbell.
'Oh my God,' he exclaimed as he opened the door. 'You appear -'
'Hello, Harry,' I said as I passed by him and upstairs. He was just behind me. We stared at each other from opposite sides of his bedroom.
'You look fantastic.'
'Thank you,' I replied. 'May I get my belongings?'

'Yeah, yeah, certainly,' he muttered dazedly. He gave me a small bag containing my clothes and books. I pulled his rolled-up jumpers from my handbag and tossed them on his bed.
'That's everything I found in your residence.'
'OK, thank you,' he replied. 'How long are you going to be here?'
'It's the weekend. 'Me, Farly, and Soph will be staying with Hicks.'
'Oh, great,' he exclaimed. He was speaking in an unusually low tone.
'Well, send them my love,' I say. However, they are unlikely to want to hear from me.' There was a brief hush as we stared at each other. 'I apologise for -'
'Don't be,' I yelled.
'I am,' he replied. 'I apologise for how I handled it.'
'Honestly, don't be, you did me the world of good,' I mumbled. "Look, I've even grown my nails, I no longer bite them, I've had my first ever manicure, would you believe it, and it only cost five quid," I said, aggressively reaching out my hands to him. Outside, I heard a car honking. Farly flapped around trying to stop Sophie and Hicks from drinking tinnies and beeping the horn.
'I've got to get going,' I said.
'Sure,' he said. We strolled down the steps in silence, and he unlocked his front door.
'Are you okay?' he inquired. 'You appear to be -'
'Thin?' I inquired.
'Yeah.'
'I'm alright, Harry,' I responded, giving him a quick hug. 'Goodbye.'
I nibbled at rice and drank pint after pint of beer while the girls took me out for a curry to celebrate what they regarded as the big conclusion of the whole miserable situation. I was more upset, ashamed, angry, and out of control than I had ever been. Whatever I was hoping to accomplish by visiting him had failed. I hadn't realised it. I pushed myself to lose weight as quickly as possible. My rage kept me going. As my weight began to plateau, indicating that the cogs of my metabolism were becoming confused and slowing down, I ate even less. Friends began questioning me about it, and Farly said that I was enslaved by an obsession. She tried to help me open up, but I laughed off her questions. In general, I discovered that making jokes about how little I ate was a fantastic way to get people off my back. I would bring it up first, so they realised it wasn't an issue, just a diet. And, as I kept reminding myself, I was still only a size 10. I

wasn't underweight; I simply started out large. I kept going because it was the only thing I had control over. I kept going because I just wanted to be happy, and everyone knows that being slimmer makes you happier. I persisted because society was praising me for my self-inflicted misery at every turn. I received comments and proposals, I felt more accepted by strangers, and practically all of my clothes looked amazing on me. I felt as if I had finally earned the right to be regarded seriously as a woman, and that everything prior to that had been superfluous. That I had been naive to believe I was ever deserving of affection. I had associated love with thinness, and to my dismay, this assumption was reinforced everywhere. My health was deteriorating as my stocks were increasing. The difficulty is that a lady can never be slender enough. It is not considered a significant price to pay to be constantly hungry, to restrict an entire food group, or to spend four nights a week in a Fitness First gym. You only need a nice grin, an average body type (give or take a stone), a little bit of hair, and an okay jumper to be an empirically handsome young man. The sky's the limit when it comes to becoming a desirable woman. Wax every surface of your body. Manicures should be done once a week. Every day, put on heels. Even if you work in an office, you should dress like a Victoria's Secret Angel. It's not enough to be a normal-sized woman with a little hair and a decent jumper. That is insufficient. We're taught we have to look like the women who are paid to look that way for a living. And the more flawless I tried to be, the more flaws I discovered. I was more self-assured as a size 14 than I was when I was three stone lighter. When I went naked with a new partner, I wanted to apologise for what I had to offer and provide a list of things I'd alter, like a middle-class hostess who says to her visitors, 'Oh, don't look at the carpet, the carpet's absolutely horrible, I promise it'll all change,' when she has guests over. Some of my friends' worries merged with annoyance. I would arrive at gatherings half-dressed, having not eaten anything in days, and roam around in a stupor, barely able to speak. Sabrina and AJ went travelling together, and I arrived late to their farewell party, felt too dizzy to speak to anyone, created an excuse, and departed after half an hour. I could feel myself pushing my life away, becoming increasingly absorbed in a wholly fictitious sense of control. Then, for the first time, I fell in love. When I first met Leo, I was roaming around a filthy house party in Elephant and Castle. I'd never seen a

more perfect dude. Tall and thin, with dark floppy hair, a strong jaw, dazzling eyes, a retroussé nose, and a seventies tache; a face half Josh Brolin, half James Taylor, with - and here's the best bit - no idea of his own beauty. He was a hippie doctoral student with a monobrow. We began dating shortly after that night. I knew it was serious because I didn't go to bed with him for two months, passionately wanting to make it perfect, to savour every second of time with him - not to rush anything. He lived in Camden, and after one of our evenings out, usually around four a.m., he'd accompany me to the bus stop outside Chalk Farm station, where I'd wait for the N5 to take me ten miles north to Edgware. I'd walk 45 minutes west to Stanmore, meandering through deserted streets lined with Volkswagens, watching the sun rise over the semi-detached red-brick houses, and I was happier than I'd ever dreamed I could be. One night, as we walked around Camden, he kissed me and ran his hands through my hair, feeling the bumps of my clip-in hair extensions. He snatched my heavy hair away from my face and tucked it behind my head.
'You'd look great with short hair,' he suggested.
'No way,' I said. 'When I was a teenager, I had a bob and I looked like a monk.'
'No, I'm talking quickly. You should go ahead and do it.'
'No,' I replied. 'I don't have the face for it,' she says.
'You do!' he said. 'Don't be a chicken. It's only hair.'
He had no idea that 'simply hair' was all I believed I was capable of. Just hair, collarbones, and sit-ups. 'Just' was all I'd put my energy into for the past year, and it was all I thought I was worth.
A month later, I went to the hairdresser with a photo of Twiggy, drank a shot of vodka, and shaved fifteen inches off my hair. Some of my fixation with my appearance vanished with it. It was snipped and dropped to the floor. Leo hadn't grasped my secret since I didn't want him to think I was crazy, but after a few months of dating, he changed his mind. I managed to avoid any problem involving food; I always told him I would eat breakfast later when we parted ways in the morning. Finally, a friend informed him that she believed I was ill.
'Is this a problem?' he inquired.
'It's great,' I answered, ashamed and terrified that I was about to lose the best person I'd ever met.

'Because I'm capable of doing this with you. I can assist you. But I can't love you if you can't communicate with me.'
'OK, it's been an issue,' I explained. 'However, that will change. I swear.'
I would have gone to great lengths to keep this man in my life. I loved him with terror and passion, and my love was forceful and fraught. I did not fall in love; rather, love fell on me. A ton of bricks thrown from a considerable height. I had no alternative but to let go of an addiction that was threatening to destroy everything.
As a result, I did. I read all the necessary books and saw the doctor. A stone creeped back on me slowly. I gradually became accustomed to eating properly. My health has improved. I even tried group support meetings in community centres, where the first thing they do is put a plate of biscuits in the middle of the room and argue about whose turn it is on the rota to bring the snacks the next week, which seemed about as useful to me as putting a bottle of Jack Daniel's in the middle of an AA meeting. I rediscovered my passion for cooking. I rediscovered my love of food. I spent every weekend with Leo doing both. My mother and I used to watch Fanny Cradock and Nigella Lawson together. Everyone kept telling me I looked 'healthy' every time they saw me, and I tried to dismiss the concept that this meant I was getting back into shape. The war was done, and the recovery process began. I regained control of my life. My hippie days set me free from my addiction to perfection. We'd get drunk and I'd have my hair cut even shorter. While I sat at the table squeezing limes into beers, he'd chop enormous chunks out with kitchen scissors. I eventually shaved both sides of my head, resulting in a tufty Mohawk. I lived in plimsolls and his jumpers and would go days without touching a make-up bag or a razor - a first for me. We'd spend weekends at the beach, washing our faces, bodies, and dishes in the sea. When we were bored on Sunday nights, we set up a tent in his bedroom. It was pure, unadulterated, and flawless.
But I knew deep down that I was still transforming myself at the command of a man's stare; I had simply moved to the opposite extreme of the spectrum. Leo hated it when I wore too much make-up, so I'd wipe it off on the bus on my way home after a party. I'd switch from heels to high-tops.
The weight I regained was not something I wanted to do for myself. I believe that if I hadn't found Leo, I would have continued to lose

weight, but by a stroke of luck, he was able to guide me to complete recovery. As I grew older and became more conscious of what a beautiful gift a good working body is, I felt humiliated and perplexed that I had treated mine so poorly. But it would be a lie to claim that I believe I will ever be completely free of what happened during that period, which no one ever tells you. You can reclaim your physical health by developing a sensible, balanced, and loving attitude about weight, as well as excellent daily practices. However, you must remember how many calories are in a boiled egg and how many steps burn how many calories. You can't forget your specific weight every week of the month that made up that time. You can try as hard as you can to block it out, but on bad days, it feels like you'll never be as happy as that ten-year-old sucking garish jam off her fingertips again.

CHAPTER 4
GOOSEBERRY FOOL: MY LIFE AS A THIRD WHEEL

It all started with a train trip. On a train, I always imagined something amazing happening to me. The transitional state of a lengthy voyage has always seemed to me to be the most beautiful and mystical of locations to find yourself in; marooned in a snug pod of your own thoughts, suspended in mid-air, travelling through a wodge of silent, blank pages between two chapters. A place where phones come and go and you're forced to spend time with your thoughts, figuring out what needs to be moulded and reordered. I've had some big dreams when riding trains. The clearest epiphanies or moments of gratitude have occurred to me when speeding through unknown English countryside, peering out at a bright rapeseed field, contemplating what I am leaving behind or about to approach. In 2008, I boarded a train at Paddington that would change my life forever, but not in the way I expected. It was nothing like Before Sunrise, Some Like It Hot, or Murder on the Orient Express. I didn't fall in love, or perform a raunchy, boozy rendition of 'Runnin' Wild' on the ukulele, or become entangled in a murder mystery; instead, I started a chain of events that would unfold slowly over the next five years, until the story was so far away that I couldn't touch it, let alone undo what I had started. The account of the train voyage that altered my life doesn't really interest me. It was the coldest winter I could recall (perhaps due to my love of the form-fitting bodycon dress at the time), and it began to snow as I was on the last Sunday-night train from London back to Exeter University. While other passengers groaned, sighed, and stomped about in frustration, I couldn't have found the whole event more lovely. I grabbed a bottle of cheap red wine from the First Great Western buffet carriage and returned to my seat to gaze out over the inky, silent countryside that was neatly powdered with thick snow like icing on a Christmas cake. On the seat across from me sat a young man about my age with the most beautiful face I'd ever seen. He'd been attempting to grab my attention while I'd been staring out the window, fantasising about a man on this broken-down train trying to catch mine. Finally, he caught my attention, introduced himself as Hector, and asked if he may join me for a drink. He exuded the peculiar, unwavering assurance that could only have come from a public school education. It's the assurance that comes with being granted an ancient jacket of identity at the age of thirteen - a set of house colours, a crass moniker, and a motto that can be recalled in song even after five pints. It's the brazen confidence that comes from being in a debating society at thirteen, then eventually elbowing its way to the top of government; the type that makes you believe it has a right to be here and things to say. Hector, fortunately, had the attributes of a cherub: dazzling blue eyes with cornflower irises and an upturned nose resembling a boy in a 1950s soap commercial. He had the curling, floppy hair of a young Hugh Grant, as well as the rich, plummy, humorous voice. We talked for two hours as the train remained motionless, laughing and drinking and eating the mince pies my mother had packed for me.

I know what you're thinking: if only this experience had been more quaint. That was also going through my nineteen-year-old mind. So, inspired by the numerous romcoms shown on terrestrial television on a Sunday night, I believed it would be a fortuitous act if we didn't exchange numbers and hoped to be reunited by coincidence. And off he went, into the chilly night at Bristol station, leaving me with enough fodder for at least three pieces on my rambling, anonymous single girl's travels' blog. I was standing at the bar in a pub on Portobello Road two years later, a few months after Harry and I had broken up, when he walked in. His cherubic face had turned sardonic and sensual when matched with a grown-up suit and coat and a slightly less floppy haircut, despite only two years of age.

'Of all the pubs in the world,' he remarked, kissing me on both cheeks as he approached me. We spent the night drinking cheap red wine while the snow fell fiercely outside and, come last orders, we were stranded once more. The snow was too heavy for me to catch a bus home, and I was too inebriated to play hard to get. He tossed me over his shoulder like a Persian shawl, unable to face the snow in an unsteady, cheap pair of heels, and we returned to his flat. We were still awake at four a.m., nude on his floor, smoking American Spirits and flicking ash into a cup resting on my stomach. He took my eyeliner from my bag and scribbled a passage from a Ted Hughes poem on his wall ('Her eyes wanted nothing to get away / Her gaze nailed down his hands, wrists, and elbows'). The phrases were smeared, smudged, and draped in kohl next to multiple charcoal sketches of a naked woman. ('I completed them. 'They're my ex,' he claimed as I lay naked as his newest project, staring up at his wall of shag memorabilia. 'Sweet girl, too bad she's married.') There was a black leather address book next to his bed with three words etched in gold on the front: BLONDES, BRUNETTES, REDHEADS. You had to hand it to him - he might have been a shagger, but he was a creative shagger. Hector had all the wishes you'd use to characterise a man in a Noel Coward play: waggish, impish, boyish, caddish, rakish, roguish. I'd never met someone quite like him before. His family had titles, he wore a floor-length wolf fur coat from Russia that had belonged to his grandfather, and his clothes had boarding school labels on them. Everything in his room had been used before or was borrowed. His supervisor was the ex-toy-boy boyfriend of his ex-socialite mother, who had given this dreadful graduate a position in the City out of affection for her. I used to leave Hector in the morning and wonder what he did at work in between flouncing around in my underwear that he wore beneath his (unpressed) trousers and sending dirty emails to me from his work account all day. Our relationship was fully nocturnal because he was entirely nocturnal, like a mythological beast of the night, like the skinned wolf for his coat. We went out and got drunk in dark pubs, and we had midnight dates. I once showed up at his place naked, wearing just a trench coat. I was twenty-one and appearing alongside an overgrown, randy Just William in a Jackie Collins novel. He never met my friends, and I never met him, which was great with us. I had no idea he had housemates until I wandered into the kitchen naked one morning at six a.m. and was greeted by a man named Scott. I slammed the door open and turned on the light to find him seated in his suit, eating cereal and reading the newspaper before going to work. Hector found it amusing - more than amusing, he liked the prospect of his housemate seeing me naked in the face exciting. We were in the first row. Scott reappeared in his dressing robe a few days later while I was making scrambled eggs in his kitchen. He gave me an apologetic smile.

'Hello,' he murmured awkwardly, waving.

'Hello,' I said. 'I'm really sorry about the previous morning. Hector informed me that no one was present. I was furious with him.'

'It's all right. To be honest, it's fine.'
'It's not fine, it's terrible, I'm very sorry,' I mumbled. 'It's the last thing you want to see before going to work.'
'It was... umm... a pleasant surprise,' he remarked. As an olive branch, I offered him some eggs and toast.
We sat and had a nice chat before broaching the subject of dating. Was he dating someone? No. Did I have any attractive single friends for him to date? Yes, I had the ideal woman. Farly, my best pal.
'But she isn't looking for a relationship right now; she's ok being single, so it would be more of a casual thing,' I warned.
'That sounds ideal.'
'Great! I'll give you her contact information. It's the least I could do,' I explained. I entered her phone number into his phone. So why not? He appeared to be a great guy - beautiful and friendly. She was presumably looking for a fling. I mentioned it to her in passing and then forgot about it. I think it's vital that I halt here to explain why I'm going to single-white-female my way through the rest of this story. Farly and I didn't hit it off right away; she spent her first year at school tethered to a clique of Power Princesses. They were a certain type of North London suburban girl who ruled the school. They wore blonde highlights, Tiffany jewellery, and stories from Brady, an Edgware social and sports organisation for Jewish youngsters; the Chinawhite of the suburbs. On the weekends, I wore all black and spent my time at school developing performances in the drama department, attempting to represent the trauma of a plane crash using only a wooden block. But when we were assigned to the same French and maths classes, we discovered we shared a sense of humour and a love of The Sound of Music and watermelon lip balms. After a few months of sitting next to each other in lessons, our after-hours friendship began tentatively. I invited her to my house first, and my mother prepared roast chicken. My father did what he does with all my pals when he is desperate to find a common language and brings up information about them in every other sentence. Farly's specialty is anything Jewish or Judaism, which he has been doing for around ten years, stating stuff like "Have you seen Sir Alan Sugar has had to downsize Amstrad?" Great pity' or 'I recently noticed an advertisement for discounted flights to Tel Aviv. It must be beautiful and hot there right now.' We were inseparable after a rough start. We spent every time we could at school together,

and when we came home, we wolfed down our dinners before calling each other to go over any other business we missed at our many meetings throughout the day. This practice has become so established that I can recall Farly's mother's phone number from 2000 to 2006 faster than I can remember my credit card PIN. I despised school and was frequently in trouble. After a suspension, a fight with my deputy head, and a detention, I returned to geography studies with a teacher who despised me. We were requested to bring our exercise books, which I had forgotten to pack, as I did with everything as a kid. I was a complete failure. A garbage bag was awarded as 'The Dolly Alderton Prize for Disorganization' at the Christmas dinner every year. The chosen student was required to go around the school and collect all of her possessions that had been left laying around. I despised it.

'Where is your practice book?' the teacher said, her unpleasant breath curdled with Nescafé and smoke.

'I forgot,' I grumbled.

'Oh, there's a surprise,' she exclaimed, raising her voice to a public announcement volume and striding around the classroom. 'She forgot about it. Is there ever a day when you haven't forgotten something? It's only one book, and it's not tough.' She smacked her board rubber against her desk. My face flushed, and I felt the discomfort that comes with holding heated tears at the back of my throat. Farly grasped my palm hard and fast beneath the table. I knew exactly what it meant. I'm here, I love you, in universal, silent Morse code. I understood at that point that everything had changed: we had transitioned. We had chosen one another. We were like family. Farley and I had always been each other's plus one on every single day of our lives. At every family dinner, holiday, and celebration, we were each other's sidekicks. We've never rowed properly unless we were boiling drunk on a night out. We've never lied to one another. I've never gone more than a few hours without thinking about her in over fifteen years. I only make sense with her as a counterbalance, and vice versa. Without Farly's affection, I'm just a jumble of ragged and half-finished ideas; of blood and muscle and skin and bone and unattainable goals and a stack of shitteen poetry under my bed. My disarray only gets shape when that familiar and favourite element of my life stands beside me. We remember the names of all our grandparents and childhood toys, and we know the exact words that will make each other laugh, cry, or shout when said in a certain order. She hasn't left a stone on the shore of my history untouched. She knows where everything is in me, and I know where everything is in her. She is, in a nutshell, my best friend. February 14th, 2010. Scott and Fairly chose that day for their first date. Who, after all, does that? I'm not sure why they bothered with a date; I thought the drink was just a formality; what they were really doing was meeting up for a one-night stand.

'I realise it sounds strange,' she admitted. 'But we've been texting for a while, and it's the only day we can both do.'

'What are your plans?'

'I'm not sure. He's going to pick me up from work and has recommended a beautiful restaurant in Notting Hill for dinner.'

'DINNER?' I demanded. 'What brings you out for bloody DINNER? 'I thought it was going to be a shag?'

'Well, I can't just walk over to his house, Doll; I have to talk to him first.'

'Yeah, but why dinner? We're not... forty. What a squandering of resources. Also, why is Valentine's Day celebrated?'

'I warned you we'd have to wait for ages because we're both so busy,' she says.

' "We're both very busy," I said. 'You're behaving as if you're married.'

'Oh, stop talking.'

'Don't you think it'll be strange when he - a man you've never seen - greets you at work and then takes you to DINNER on VALENTINE'S DAY surrounded by LOADS OF COUPLES? 'Don't you think it'll cloud your judgement about whether you like him or not?'

'No. It will be really informal.'

The meal went great. The dinner was far from casual. Scott picked Farly up from Harrods, where she was working on a jewellery counter in the rain (in the rain - Christ, talk about gilding the lily); they took a cab to Notting Hill, went to the restaurant, and Fairly had the best date of her life. Farly didn't do her typical thing of wittering on and on about how it was the finest date of her life, so I knew it was the best date of her life. She was evasive when I asked her about Scott. Measured. She even sounded a little mature. The irritating adultery of Fairly and Scott's engagement made me realise how far my relationship with Hector had fallen. Hector's 'wishes' went off like milk - selfish, oafish, and frightening. I didn't want to drink a bottle of white wine for breakfast, hit him over the head with a loafer in a play fight, or pretend to be a naughty pixie as part of his fanciful, overcomplicated storyline in his sexual dreams because he was too disastrous. He got drunk, passed out, and locked me out of his house for the better part of a night twice in a week. The ideal head-boy confidence came with another requirement: a matron. And that was not my assignment.

'Please, Dolly,' Farly implored as he pleaded for a Friday night out. 'Please, just one more night with him, please.'

'No,' I answered emphatically. 'I don't like him any longer.'

'Oh, but Scott and I aren't at the point where I can just go round to his flat without looking like a stalker.'

'You've never been concerned by it before.' (Farly once handed a man £20 in phone credit and made him pledge to SMS her if he didn't text her back; he never did.)

'Yes, but I want to be normal with him,' she explained firmly. 'I'm acting normal with him, which is quite great. Please contact Hector via text. It won't be awkward if we go around together.' I considered it. 'Come on, I did it for you.'

She had damned her to damnation. I texted Hector to let him know I was bringing Fairly. We boarded a late-night bus to Notting Hill.

The pair of them went off after the four of us had a drink together in their living room, Hector droning on about the history of nipple clamps in his obnoxious, drunk Nigel Havers voice while Fairly did her best hair-twirling and shy smile at Scott. Hector escorted me up to his bedroom so he could "show me something." He was acting unusually emotional and needy, as men like him do when they notice you've become distant (I hadn't responded to his filthy limerick emails in over two weeks). I sat on his bed, drinking warm white wine from the bottle.

'What exactly is it?' I asked simply. He took up guitar. Oh no. Not this, not anything else. The bedroom I had spent months fantasising about and wishing I could be in had suddenly turned into a cave of my own particular nightmares. I noticed the bohemian mess for what it was: soiled socks scattered over the floor, a subtle stench of mould and dust that smelled like an old cricket pavilion on a damp day, and a comforter with holes burned from unconscious chain smoking. The lovely charcoal of naked women had mutated into ominous, knowing gargoyles gazing down at me. We had to go through that, and now you have to as well, they snarled.

'There's something I want you to hear,' he mumbled, striking two furious notes in between tuning his guitar.

'Oh, no, it's okay, you don't have to.'

'Dolly Alderton,' he said, as if at an open-mic night. 'I am completely smitten. 'I wrote this song just for you.' He began playing the three chord pattern he had previously played me over and over.

In an Americana croak, he sang, "I saw her on a train." 'My life would never be the same again. We -'after the first night

'Hector,' I grumbled as I felt the alcohol strike me full force. 'I believe we should no longer see each other.'

I departed early the next morning with Farly, and I never saw him again. Farly and Scott informed me that I had truly broken his heart, and that the Mulberry Bayswater handbag of an overnight guest did not appear on the kitchen table for at least three weeks after that night.

(Footnote: Hector is now a wealthy entrepreneur married to a Hollywood actress. I learned about it from a Mail Online piece while sitting in my pyjamas eating an entire chocolate yule log to myself: go figure.)

CHAPTER 5
BEING BJÖRN AGAIN

When I stopped seeing Hector, I figured it was only a matter of time before Farly and Scott faded away. I'd been the glue that held them together, and when I left that filthy block of flats in Notting Hill, I figured they'd have little in common anymore. But, after a few weeks, Farly casually mentioned that they were going on a mini-break to Cambridge. Jealousy surged through my veins, stinging my entire body like vinegar. I was the one who had always had a boy around, and suddenly she was the one with a legitimate, older partner. Not one who had her wear her knickers to work, who forced her wear a fishnet body stocking, who didn't know her surname, or who contacted her only once a week. Farly had a lover who spent more time with her while she was sober than when she wasn't, who took her on mini-breaks, called her instead of texting, and wanted to have real talks with her.
'What is there even in Cambridge?' I screamed angrily at AJ. 'How about Bella Italia? So, best of luck. Have a good time.'
'How does he seem?' AJ inquired. The reality is, I didn't know much.
'Bad news,' I remarked solemnly. 'She's too elderly and serious for her.'
And then, almost three months later, he told her he loved her. She revealed it at a dinner with friends. We all toasted it and yelled with delight; on the night bus home, I wrote a sorrowful soliloquy about it on my iPhone notes. Despite how much I despised watching Farly be mistreated by ignorant adolescent lads throughout the years - being led on, ignored, and dumped - I recognized there was a safety in it. As long as no boys took serious notice of her, I had her all to myself. I was completely fucked the moment a grown-up man with a brain stopped and showed interest in her. He couldn't help but fall in love with her. She was lovely and amusing. She was the sweetest person I knew, having spent years loaning me money to bail me out of trouble and picking me up at three a.m. in her car when my bus home had broken down. She was built of the stuff that would make an ideal partner: she put people first, listened, and remembered things. She wrote messages in my packed lunch box before I went to work and sent cards to express her pride in me. I had always attracted boys by

using smoke and mirrors, exaggeration and bravado, heavy make-up, and excessive drinking. There was no acting or lying with Farly - if a boy ended up adoring her, he adored every cell of her from the first date, whether he realised it or not. She had been my best-kept secret, and now it had been revealed. The following year, we had our first row since adolescence at a Christmas gathering at our friend Diana's house. I was with Leo at the time. She and Scott arrived late, and it was the first time I'd seen her in a month. I made no outward attempt to greet her, instead watching them from the corner of my eye. I made a point of laughing very loudly at really unfunny things just to let her know I was there and having a good time without her. The talk was stilted and abrupt when she arrived.

'Why have you been neglecting me this evening?' she eventually inquired.

'How come you've ignored me for a year?' I responded.

'What do you mean, I texted you yesterday?'

'Texting, yes. You're fantastic at texting. Texting is your "get out of jail free" card, which means you don't have to see me for months on end and go to Scott's flat every night because you can claim, "Oh, but I text her." Every day, I text her.'

'Can we do it upstairs?' she demanded.

I stomped up to Diana's room, refilled my plastic cup with Glen's vodka and a splash of Coke. We yelled at each other for two hours. We started out loud, then went quieter, until we were too angry and tired to go on, at which point we made up. I told her she'd left me; I made up a sophisticated metaphor about how I'd learned she'd always thought of me as Björn Again.

'WHAT DOES THAT MEAN?' she exclaimed.

'Björn once more. They were the opening act for the Spice Girls show, which we both attended. They were terrible, and we couldn't wait for it to end. I realised I'd been your warm-up act for the past eleven years until your headliner arrived. You've NEVER been my warm-up act, you've ALWAYS been my Spice Girls, and I wish I'd known sooner so I could have put you on the bill and MADE YOU BURN AGAIN.'

She told me I was overreacting and that she was allowed to have her first relationship. I told her she could have her first boyfriend; I just didn't expect her to prioritise him over everyone else. We emerged with our faces smeared like Jackson Pollock splatter canvases with a bucket of mascara. Scott and Leo stood at the bottom of the stairs in quiet, evidently out of football and light current affairs conversation. We got our coats and walked away separately. Diana later told me that they had turned down the music downstairs so that the entire party could hear the disagreement.

'He's her boyfriend,' my infuriatingly reasonable academic boyfriend said as we drank tinnies on the long walk back to his Stockwell flat. 'They've fallen in love, and she's transformed. That's okay; it's all part of growing up.'

'You're my boyfriend,' I said angrily. 'I'm madly in love. I've not changed. She remains the most significant person in my life. She is still the person I most want to see. I don't put my connection first.'

He drank a gulp from his beer can.

'Perhaps that's not usual,' he replied.

Leo and I split up after two years together. I had tried everything I could to make it work, but so much had changed since we met as undergraduates at a house party in Elephant and Castle. We'd both matured and become very different people. I had drifted from magazine to newspaper as an unpaid chair-filler under the pretence of a work experience placement for nine long months after finishing journalistic training. I'd been turned down for positions as an intern at Tatler, an editorial assistant at Weight Watchers, and a waitress at a nearby Pizza Express. To sustain myself, I went back to my previous job as a promo girl, walking down previous Brompton Road with a bunch of out-of-work West End dancers and air hostesses, handing out fliers for a rib restaurant. I quit after being accosted by anti-fur protesters outside Harrods while dressed as a pig. I was in severe need of work. It was all I could think of from the moment I woke up until I fell asleep in my childhood bedroom. I craved a job in my early twenties with the same zeal that I craved my first boyfriend in my early teens, obsessed over who I knew who had one and grilling them on the specifics of how they got one. Night after night, lying in bed, thinking how many more years this could go on for. Finally, I was standing on a train platform one early evening when I received a call from an unknown number. Tim, a story producer for E4's upcoming structured reality show Made in Chelsea, answered the phone. I had written a series of internet evaluations of the first season that the production company had read and found hilarious (again, paid in the post-grad currency of 'exposure' - this time it actually worked). He invited me to their East London office to discuss a possible creative role on the show. Tim and Dilly, the thirty-something, teeny-tiny, fresh-faced BAFTA-winning executive producers, interviewed me. They explained that they had seen my assessment of the final episode, which included some sarcastic recommendations to the show's creators on how to improve the future series. Dan, the company's owner, had researched every review on the internet after becoming famous in the 1990s as the producer and co-host of a phenomenally successful late-night chat show. When he found mine, he printed copies for all the producers, who read it on their way to a meeting with the channel - and, to their surprise, they agreed with everything. I left my first half-hour interview with Dilly and Tim feeling relieved that I might never hear from them again. I had no idea what they were pursuing, and we spent the majority of the interview examining rich people's routines and psychoanalysing the actors. We didn't discuss my qualifications, employment history, or job needs at all. I had no idea that correct psychoanalysis accounts for 90% of the success of reality television. And my years of watching affluent people's behaviour while feeling on the outside of their club - standing in boarding school tuck shops and smoking areas of King's Road nightclubs - would, for the first time, over-qualify me for a job. Three days later, while at a music festival with Leo, I received the second call from the series producer. We'd taken on the role of our camping party's Official Glitter Appliers with gusto. A high schooler heard continuous ringing emanating from my tent and assumed it was Kraftwerk performing a surprise set. It was, indeed, Dilly. She told me I'd been hired as the show's story producer and to come in the next day for my first meeting. I arrived at the office without showering for four days, my nose sunburned, and my white-blonde pixie hair matted into a Mohawk. While I went to my first story meeting, Leo waited in reception with our backpacks and tent. I was out of clean clothing, so I dressed up in Leo's oversized T-shirt, denim jacket, laddered tights, and ballet pumps. The attire was an appropriate send-off: it was my final day as a child and my first day as an adult. I fell in love with my new job's creativity, humour, and relentlessness, as well as my new colleagues and supervisors, almost as furiously as I had with Leo. When I wasn't in the office or on site, I started doing freelance journalism, so I could write in the evenings and on weekends, which

left me with little to no time for anything else, much to Leo's chagrin. He felt a little duped. He'd fallen in love with a rootless girl who wanted nothing more than to pack a bag of plimsolls and jeans and go on any adventure he took her on; who embroidered his initials into jumpers and spent the entire night with him locked in a bathroom, sitting in the empty bath, staring at his face with saucer eyes. He ended up with a woman who had her own adult personality and was obsessed with her profession. I felt that our relationship had been one of the most fulfilling experiences of my life, and I knew he'd always be a big part of who I'd become, but we'd outgrown each other. I felt I had to let him go so he could be with someone who genuinely wanted to be in a relationship with him and give him all the love and dedication he deserved. Farly, AJ, and I were finally out of our suburban houses and into our first London apartment. AJ, too, had recently divorced. Farly remained with Scott. A part of me hoped that by living with two single women, Farly would realise what she'd been missing her entire twenties and end her relationship with Scott. But, if anything, living with AJ and me made her appreciate him even more. She once saw me run around getting ready for a first date, trim some fresh fake eyelashes, apply them, then scream in agony as I realised I had used the kitchen scissors I had used the night before to slice chillies over a pizza. She found a package of frozen potato smiley faces and placed them in front of my eyes as I contacted the guy to cancel. 'God, I don't miss this,' she said, sighing. Farly, AJ, and I had been out dancing in our favourite Camden dive club one night while Scott was gone on business. We arrived home and opened an old bottle of Tia Maria, and things got confessional in the way that they often do in the aftermath of a night out.'I miss Scott,' Farly said as she sipped the rest of her Tia Maria.
'Why?' I exclaimed. AJ fixed his gaze on me. 'I mean, he's only gone for a few days,' she says.
'I understand, but I still miss him while he's gone. And every time I see him, I feel aroused. I'm looking forward to hearing the front door open again, even if he only goes to the corner store and returns.' She noticed my scowl. 'It may sound corny, but it's true.'
'I think she truly likes him,' I told myself the next day.
'Of course she likes him,' AJ murmured as he lay on the couch, nibbling on a bacon sandwich. 'How come they've been together for three years?'

'I'm not sure. I assumed she was just curious about what it was like to have a boyfriend.'

AJ shook her head, stunned. 'Come on, buddy.'

After I discovered this, I began to notice subtle signs everywhere. Scott and Farly's parents met. Farly was spending more and more weekends with his adult pals, doing adult things like 'thirtieth birthday weekends in the Cotswolds' and wine tasting on a weekday. Scott came around a lot, which I despised. And I despised it when he wasn't around. He was doomed to fail. I didn't want him to triumph.

CHAPTER 6
THE UNCOOL GIRLS OF UNCOOL CAMDEN

I went out for a drink with a friend on a Tuesday night after work when I was twenty-four, during my first year in London with Fairly and AJ. Despite my efforts to hold her out till last orders, she had to leave at half eight because she had an early meeting the next morning. I texted everyone in my phonebook who I thought could be nearby and wanted to spend the night with me, but everyone was busy, in bed, or weary. I sulked my way home on the 24 bus, my beloved steed that whisked me from the heart of London to just outside my door in twenty minutes, feeling restless and upset that I couldn't stay out for just one more hour and one more glass of wine. It's a feeling I'd grown accustomed to: panicked and throaty; a sense that everyone else in London was having a good time but me; that there were pots of experiential gold hidden on every street corner and I wasn't finding them; that one day I'd die, so why end any potentially perfect and glorious day with an early night?
When the 24 arrived at the bar at the end of my street, I snapped out of my funk. It was a NW5 shack, a once-famous music venue turned drab boozer for Camden's nine a.m. drinkers. I stepped off the bus and entered. It was the first time I'd come since the day we moved in, when we were told Farly had made history by being the first customer to order a coffee in forty years. The landlord walked across the street to the corner shop and charged her 26p for some Nescafé Gold Blend and milk. I ordered a beer and struck up a conversation with the bartender, who appeared unsurprised to be serving yet another single drinker. A man in his late sixties with a grey yeti beard next to me inquired about my day, and I regretted the lack of a drinking companion to accompany me through the night. He claimed to be the right man for the job. As we drank, he told me about his childhood in the area: the school he'd skipped, how things had changed, the drinking holes that had closed; the John Martyn concert he'd seen at the Camden Palace before I was born, the live recordings of which I had compulsively listened to. I departed at midnight, scrawling the man's phone number on the back of a beer mat with the

mutual promise that we'd spend an afternoon listening to records together, but knowing I'd never hear from him again. He was only 'a night,' and I wanted a lot of them. A story, an anecdote, a fresh face, a recollection. He was a piece of advice, a gossipy story, and an interesting fact that became lodged in my inebriated, unconscious mind, only to be extracted and regurgitated as my own one day. Someone might inquire, "Where did you hear that?" I'd respond, "I have no idea."

When I got home from work the next night with an unmovable hangover and found Fairly and AJ snuggled up on the sofa, I told them how I'd ended up in a shabby bar down the road the night before.

'How could you have done that?' AJ inquired, puzzled.

'Because it was Tuesday evening,' I explained. 'I could, too.'

I am pleased that I fetishized the measured-out-in-coffee-spoons minutiae of maturity as a teenager, because the relief of finally arriving meant that I considered very little of it to be a hardship. I've enjoyed being able to pay my own rent. Every day, I've enjoyed cooking for myself. I used to get a rush sitting in the GP's waiting room, knowing that I had registered and gotten myself there without the assistance of anyone else. I'd fall weak in the knees over a letter from Thames Water written to me in my first year of bill-paying. I would gladly accept the administrative burden that comes with being an adult in exchange for the knowledge that I can always go to the pub on my own and make friends with an old man any day of the week. I've never been able to get over the fact that I no longer have to sip gin from shampoo bottles; that there is no lights-out; and that I can stay up watching movies or writing until four a.m. on a weeknight if I want to. I'm relieved, motivated, and stimulated that I can eat breakfast foods for dinner, listen to records loudly, and smoke a cigarette out my window. I still can't believe my good fortune. My entire life as a young twenty-something adult was spent like Macaulay Culkin in Home Alone 2: Lost in New York, who finds himself booked at The Plaza and orders mounds of ice cream from room service while watching gangster flicks. This is totally due to my rigorous upbringing. Almost every adult I've encountered who went to boarding school couldn't believe they could go to a Kentish Town old man's bar on a Tuesday night and not be given detention, suspension, or rustication, whatever that means. If university had been a playground for me to act out my grownup ambitions, having my own property and salary in London was akin to utopia. We looked for our first adult London house for three months. Our budget was limited, and flats with three double bedrooms were difficult to come across. There was the house in Finsbury Park that looked like a Notting Hill mews house but was actually a wing of Pentonville Prison ('All we'd do here is stay in and watch The X Factor while eating Sainsbury's Basics penne,' AJ joked). Farly and AJ attended a catastrophic showing of a property on the estate in Brixton, along with a large throng of millennial aspirants who queued outside like it was Madame Tussauds. The estate agent failed to bring the keys, so they had to wait for half an hour, then after a three-minute tour of the dump and leaving, they all had to drop down to the ground because a shooter was on the loose and being hunted by police outside the property. Finally, just as we were about to give up, Farly discovered a three-bed in our price range through a private landlord on Gumtree. It was located off a notoriously sketchy crescent that connected Camden Town's Chalk Farm and Kentish Town ends. It had a true old-fashioned market twice a week where you could buy pairs of five-pound slippers and cartoon bed linens, a daily fruit and vegetable stall, and a cash-only independent store where you could buy cannabis from under the sandwich counter. It was brazen, brash, and stunning. The house was a lovely shambles. One of a row of 1970s ex-council maisonettes made of Lego-yellow bricks with odd window and door arrangement and proportions that made it look like it was created in a hurry by a teenager playing The Sims. The front garden had two overgrown shrubs that meant you couldn't go through the old wooden front gate without active arm-swiping in the summer. The kitchen tiles were decorated with motifs from the English countryside. The back garden was a weedy jungle. There were these strange liquid streak stains down the hallway wall that we could only presume were piss after considerable investigation. Everything smelled damp. Squatters were living in the flat above us. Gordon, the landlord, was a well-dressed man in his forties with a boxy midlife crisis leather jacket and strangely dark, floppy hair. He was also a BBC news presenter, and he wanted everyone to know it: his voice was loud and pompous, and his demeanour was strangely harsh and informal.

'This is the hallway,' Gordon exclaimed. 'As you can see, there's a lot of storage space.' We walked through one of the enormous dusty white doors. A black box rested in the middle of the empty shelves, inscribed with the words 'RAT ATTACK!' in a large yellow typeface. 'Oh, disregard that,' he murmured, taking it in his palm. 'Everything is now in order.' We exchanged glances for a few seconds. 'Do you know what?' he asked, gently wrinkling his nose. 'I think the best thing is that I just stay out of your way and let you explore the place on your own. 'Please let me know when you've viewed everything.'

It was quirky, wobbly, and strange, but we knew it would be the ideal first home not only for us, but also for our extended family of friends, whom we wanted to entertain every weekend. We walked back downstairs to tell Gordon we wanted it because he was on the phone.

'Ya... ya... well. That's the worst-case scenario,' he replied dismissively, flailing his fingers at us. 'Ya. For the time being, let's just keep it out of court. I don't want to go back there.' He rolled his eyes as he stared at us. 'Great, so I'll be around tomorrow at 10 to examine this roof. OK. Yap. OK. Yes, yes, yes. OK. Bye.' He slid his phone into the rear pocket of his jeans. 'Bloody renters,' he called them. 'Do you want it or do you not want it?'

We scrimped and saved to cover our deposits, so the first month was spent in frenzied, thrilling frugality. We didn't have much for the house, so Farly purchased a pack of Post-its to attach on various surfaces and write stuff like 'TV WILL BE HERE' or 'TOASTER WILL BE HERE'. Every night for dinner, we ate Marmite and cucumber sandwiches. On the second night in our new home, I arrived to find both of the girls running around the living room in their wellies because they'd seen the first mouse and didn't want it to run over their bare feet as they tried to capture it. Farly purchased a block of Pilgrims Choice Cheddar from the Nisa Local, placed it in her empty vanity case, and waggled it on the carpet, attempting to lure the mouse to a safe rescue. We also quickly became acquainted with the manager of the neighbourhood corner shop, Ivan, a middle-aged man with the physique of a marine. On our initial visit, he ominously warned us that if we "fell into any trouble with any gangs," we should come to him right away because it would be "dealt with." Farly was wearing a pearl necklace at the time. But I felt weirdly safer knowing Ivan was always ten seconds' walk from our front door and that if the mouse thing became a reoccurring issue, he was always there to help. I'd frequently jump out of the house barefoot in my jammies and into the shop, crying 'IT'S BACK, IVAN!' 'IT'S BACK!' said Blanche DuBois-style.

'All right, dahlingin', all right,' he'd say. 'I'll be there right away. 'Would you like me to bring my gun?' I'd decline and ask him to bring his torch instead, and he'd crouch under every bed, fridge, and sofa in search of it.

(Gordon eventually arranged for an exterminator to come in. An East End old man with the surname 'Mouser,' ironically. I asked him whether there was a more humanitarian method to deal with the situation after he set some traps.

'No,' he murmured, his arms folded in disappointment.

'OK,' I said. 'I'm just a vegetarian,' she says.

'You don't have to eat it,' he said.)

Camden seemed like the ideal location for us: it was central, close to all of the best parks, and, most of all, it was dangerously, hopelessly uncool. Nobody our age lived there, nor did any of our pals. We encountered swarms of Spanish students on a school trip or forty-something men with Paul Weller hairstyles and winkle-picker shoes who were still waiting for Camden's glory years of Britpop to return. AJ used to refer to it as "Goon Watch." On a Saturday night, we'd walk along the High Street, and she'd slur 'Goon, goon, goon' in my ear, pointing at passers-by. For the first few months I lived there, I had a gorgeous but ultimately ruinously self-obsessed musician boyfriend who lived in East London and refused to visit me because Camden was 'too 2007'.

Occasionally, during our time there, we'd go to an East London party or a night out and be surrounded by young, cool, handsome people, and we'd question whether this was where we were supposed to be at our age. But, as we left, we were always fatigued by the experience and thankful that we lived somewhere where we didn't have to pretend we were cooler than we were. We could go shopping in our leggings and hoodies without running into anyone we knew. We could take over a dance floor in a line doing a drunken, hilarious cancan and still be the coolest people in the entire bar. We could go out and spend the entire evening engrossed in one other without attempting to impress anyone. There was literally no one left to impress in Camden. One of the first things I purchased for the house was a soup kitchen-sized cooking pot. Our guests had always been terrific eaters, and I was overjoyed to have my own stove and kitchen table. We had folks around for supper three times a week throughout our first year together. I figured out what was the cheapest to make - pot after pot of dhal, tray after tray of Parmigiana. In the summer, we'd have candlelit dinners in our terribly overgrown garden; at one point, it was so overgrown that a tree caught fire in an oddly biblical fashion, and we all drunkenly splashed saucepans of water and glasses of Ivan's terrible five-pound Sauvignon Blanc over it. There was a sense of liberation in the realisation that our house was fundamentally too broken to repair. Gordon was also unconcerned; he let us paint all the walls bright colours and never complained when the paint dried with a wobbly line on the stairway wall, where we had reached the bottom of the Dulux tin. It meant it was a house we could live in, not one we were overly attached to. We could destroy it on a Saturday night, and all it would take the next morning was a ten-minute tidy to make it look passable again. We could play our records loudly and stay up till six a.m. without the neighbours complaining - I think those 1970s houses were intended to be disco-proof, because we never received a single noise complaint in the years we lived there. In fact, the neighbour stated that she had never heard us. As a result, our residence was also a place where people might come to get high. In my first couple of years in London, I got the majority of my drug experimenting out of my system. First, I established a familial bond with Fergus, a friendly drug dealer. Fergus wasn't a moodily-sit-in-the-car-and-pass-you-a-baggie-under-the-dashboard dealer, but rather would join me late on a Friday night when I had friends over for dinner, rolling spliffs at the table and telling long-winded jokes while digging into the leftovers, before I'd send him packing with a Tupperware box of spaghetti carbonara. Farly, who had always been much more sensible than me and was always in bed by midnight when we had friends over for supper, had never met Fergus but was always perplexed by the way I spoke about him as if he were 'a cousin or a family acquaintance'. She was awakened at four a.m. one night by the sound of me giving Fergus a walking tour of the house while he advised me on the feng shui of each room. She walked into my room the next day to find me huffing and puffing while transferring my bed to the opposite wall.

'What are you up to?' she inquired.
'I'm relocating my bed. According to Fergus, he is not in a good position right now.'
'Because the headboard is too close to the radiator,' she says. He claims that being near heat is bad for your head, especially your sinuses.'
'Yeah, Dolly, the man sells you Class A drugs,' Farly added. 'He's not in a position to give medical advice.'
Fergus abruptly dropped out of contact, as I was told they frequently do, so I was directed to CJ, who was a steadfast catastrophe. CJ was known as London's worst drug dealer. His timekeeping was abysmal; he would frequently deliver the 'wrong order' to the 'wrong customer' and then show up at your house half an hour later demanding the 'stuff' back. His phone had never been charged. His GPS was constantly failing. He'd kept me waiting for an hour and a half, and I found myself telling him over the phone, like an angry teacher, that he was "his own worst enemy." The final straw came on the Thursday before I left London for a festival, when I called him and asked if he could sell me some MDMA.
'What is that?' he inquired.
'MDMA,' I said. 'Mandy.'
'Who exactly is she?'
'Ecstasy. Come on, people. MDMA.'
'I'd never heard of it,' he admitted.
No matter how I obtained them or who gave them to me, the process of getting them was almost always more fascinating than the drugs themselves. Talking about whether to get any, dialling the number, withdrawing the money; someone waiting in the flat while someone else went to get the car, returning with a tiny plastic pocket of herbs or powder; the promise of what was to come - that was the part that had my heart racing the fastest. Farly once witnessed the work required to purchase, split, and consume cocaine and couldn't believe how time-consuming it was; 'Like making a shepherd's pie,' she observed. However, for someone who never wants a night to end, the time-consuming faff of lining up powder and rolling up spliffs is the whole fun of it - it's a distraction, a guaranteed night extension. It is your rational mind's muting that says Go to bed at eleven o'clock, we've talked about all there is to speak about now, and in its place is an artificial desire for the party to last forever. Cocaine was always

just a way for me to keep drinking and staying awake long after I was exhausted; I was never that into any sensation it provided.

I used to believe that in order to be a writer, you had to gather experiences. And I used to believe that every worthwhile experience, every worthwhile person, existed only after dark. I always remembered something Hicks said to me as we lay in bed with the fairy lights flashing around her window.

'One day, Dolly, we'll be sitting in a nursing home, bored out of our minds and looking at the quilt on our laps,' she said. 'And all we'll have to make us happy will be these memories.'

However, the increasing frequency of these nights meant that I felt defined by these stories rather than a specialist collector of them. Staying out until dawn became a regular occurrence for me, and I grew to associate any evening out with a hedonistic all-nighter. Worse, everyone else expected it of me as well. Friends expected that consistent level of debauchery from me, even when we met up for a simple pad thai on a Thursday evening. My energy, bank account, and mental state couldn't keep up. And I didn't want to make myself into some terrible Village Drunk figure, with whom everyone would dread having coffee, knowing that it would surely finish the next morning in some all-night casino in Leicester Square.

'I adore those stories,' Helen said one morning after we'd been to a party and I'd gathered a crowd to bore them with my best folkloric tales of evenings out. 'But, Doll, there are a lot of them.'

Another thing no one tells you about drinking as you get older is that the severe paranoia and dread in the sober hours of the next day became a typical part of my mid-twenties. The gap between who you were on a Saturday night, commandeering an entire pub garden by shouting obnoxiously about how you've always felt you had at least three prime-time sitcom scripts in you, and who you are on a Sunday afternoon, thinking about death and worrying about whether the postman likes you or not, becomes too large. Growing up brings about self-awareness. And self-awareness kills a self-proclaimed party girl cold.

I also ended up with two very unrelated occupations, working in television and as a freelance writer. They demanded more and more of my time and attention, and regular binge drinking and hangovers were counterproductive to productivity and creativity. 'You're attempting to live two lives,' a buddy once said to me when I was on the verge of collapse. 'You have to decide if you want to be the lady who parties the hardest or the woman who works the hardest.'

I choose to aim for the latter. Life became more interesting during the day, and there was less need to flee at night. But it would take some time for me to discover that the path to adventure does not only involve late nights, hot pubs, cold wine, strangers' flats, parked cars with lights on, and small bags of powder. I used to think of alcohol as a mode of transportation for experiencing things, but as I got older, I realised it could both stunt and intensify my experiences. Sure, there were the juicy confessionals you'd receive from folks with dilated pupils in a restroom stall; the old men with interesting stories you'd never meet otherwise; the locations you'd go; and the people you'd kiss. But there was also the work that you couldn't do while you were hungover. All the horrible impressions you'd make on potential pals because you couldn't speak because you were so inebriated. All those lost discussions in which someone tells you something extremely significant, but neither of you remembers it the next morning. All those hours spent sweating and panicking in your bed at five a.m., your heart racing as you stare at the ceiling, longing for sleep. All the hours spent tormenting yourself in your thoughts with all the idiotic things you said and did, hating yourself for the next several days.

Years later, I'd learned that consistently behaving in a way that makes you feel ashamed means you'll never be able to take yourself seriously, and your self-esteem would fall. My teenage one-woman crusade to be a grown-up through excessive drinking, however, left me feeling more like a child than any other activity in my life. For many years in my twenties, I felt as if I were about to be accused of something terrible, as if someone could easily march up to me and say, 'YOU'RE the dick who drank Jo Malone Pear and Freesia bath oil in a pint glass at my house party for a dare - you owe me £42!' I still can't believe you had an affair with my boyfriend outside the Sainsbury's on Mornington Crescent!' - I'd have to nod reverently and say, 'Yes, I can't recollect it particularly, but I'll take your word for it and apologise.' Imagine walking around in a world where you're always expecting someone to tell you you're an arsehole, and you're ready to agree wholeheartedly. What kind of entertainment is that?

From now until the day I die, wherever I go on a Tuesday night, you can be sure that I would rather be at a dismal Camden tavern sipping beer and talking to a stranger. But, like the yellow-bricked maisonette that was crumbling down, I finally grew out of those clockwork-regular blackout benders that wiped out the next day like a wave. But for a brief moment, sitting in my overgrown Eden garden with the people I loved, drinking sour Sauvignon with the record player turned up loud and empty dishes piled high by the sink, I felt I lived in the nicest house in the world. I still believe I did.

CHAPTER 7
'NOTHING WILL CHANGE'

One of the things I despised about Farly meeting Scott was that I never saw her family again. I missed her mother, father, stepmother, brother, and sister. I spent every other weekend and holiday with her family for years, and they became like my own. However, after Scott arrived on the scene, I no longer received the call-up from Farly, so I only saw them once or twice a year. Scott had taken my place at the dining-room table for birthdays and Sunday roasts; he was the one who joined them on chilly, pleasant autumnal half-terms in Cornwall while I browsed Instagram. After a few months in our new London home, Farly invited me to join her family on a Saturday afternoon walk. We stopped for lunch at a pub, and I basked in the warm familiarity of their rituals: the nicknames, inside jokes, and stories about Family and me when we were teenagers. I was smug; whatever area Scott had occupied for the last few years had a different form than mine, because nothing had changed. Due to competitive overeating at lunch, we lagged behind the rest of the group and the dog on the final leg of the walk, as we'd always done as teenagers.
'Scott has invited me to live with him.'
'What did you say?' I inquired.
'I'm going to do it,' she muttered almost regretfully, her timid words drifting into the frigid air. 'When he asked me, it felt natural.'
'When?'
'After a year with you guys in Camden,' she replied. I loathed the expression 'done a year' as if it were a gap-year ski season or a TEFL course in Japan; something you do once for a memorable narrative.
'OK,' I said.
'I'm very sorry, I know it's really difficult.'
'No, no, I'm delighted for you,' I said. The rest of the hike was spent in silence.
'Would you like to bake some chocolate chip cookies?' When we arrived back at our house, Fairly said,
'Yeah.'
'Great. Make a list of the ingredients we'll need, and I'll go get them.
'How about we watch that Joni Mitchell documentary that's been sitting on the shelf for ages?'

'Sure,' I replied. It reminded me of when I was eight years old and my mother took me to McDonald's after my goldfish died.

We sat on the sofa, our legs interlaced, our tummies peeking out from under our pyjamas, nibbling cookies. Graham Nash was referring to Blue's soul-baring lyrics.

'I know every word on that album,' I declared. When Farly passed her driving test at the age of seventeen, it was the only album we'd taken on a three-week summer road trip.

'Me too. "Carey" is my personal favourite.'

"All I Want" is now mine. I took a break to finish my cookie and remove the crumbs from my mouth. 'We'll probably never do another road trip like that.'

'Why?'

'Because you're moving in with your boyfriend, you'll be doing all of your road trips with him from now on.'

'Don't be a moron,' she warned. 'There will be no change.'

I'd like to take a brief break from the story to discuss the phrase "nothing will change." During my twenties, I heard it spoken to me often by women I care about when they moved in with boyfriends, got engaged, moved abroad, got married, or became pregnant. 'There will be no change.' It drives me insane. Everything will be altered. Everything will be altered. The affection we have for one other remains constant, but the format, tone, frequency, and intimacy of our friendship will alter indefinitely. When you were a teenager and you saw your mother with her best friends and they seemed close, but they weren't like you and your pals? When they initially met, there would be a peculiar formality between them, a tiny uneasiness. Your mother would tidy the house before they arrived, and they would discuss their children's coughs and hair-care regimens. Farly used to say to me as a kid, "Promise we'll never get like that." Promise that when we're fifty, we'll be precisely the same. I want us to sit on the couch, eating chips and talking about thrush. I don't want to become a group of women that get together once a month for a craft sale at the NEC.' I made a pledge. But I had no idea how much effort it takes to maintain that level of intimacy with a friend as you get older - it doesn't just happen. I've seen it time and again: a woman always fits better into a man's life than he does into hers. She will be the one who spends the most time at his flat, making friends with all of his buddies and their girlfriends. On his mother's birthday, she will be the one to send her a bouquet of flowers. Women despise this nonsense just as much as men do, but they're better at it - they just get on with it. This indicates that when a lady my age falls in love with a man, her priorities are as follows:

1. Family and 2. Friends

Regarding this:

1. The family
2. Husband
3. The family of the boyfriend
4. Friends of the boyfriend
5. Boyfriend's pals' girlfriends
6. Friends

That is, you move from seeing your friend every weekend to once every six weekends on average. She transforms into a baton, and you're at the very end of the track. You have your turn for a special occasion, such as your birthday or a brunch, and then you have to pass her back around to the boyfriend to begin the lengthy, dull rotation all over again. These gaps in each other's lives gradually but steadily develop a chasm in the centre of your friendship. The affection remains, but the familiarity has vanished. Before you realise it, you're no longer sharing your life. You're spending your lives apart with your men, then getting together for supper every six weekends to inform each other how life is. I now see why our mothers cleaned the house before their best friend came over and asked them, 'What's the news, then?' in a cheery, stilted tone. I understand how that happens. So don't tell me that nothing will change when you move in with your lover. There will be no road trip; the cycle also applies to vacations; I'll have my pal back every sixth summer, unless she has a baby, in which case I'll get my road trip in eighteen years. It never ceases to happen. Everything will be altered. Farly moved out on my 25th birthday. She and Scott found a one-bedroom apartment in Kilburn with a roof terrace to rent. It was right next to a gym, which they thought was ideal because they liked to play badminton. She made a big deal out of showing me a direct bus from Camden to Kilburn High Road. On the drive to their housewarming party, I sulked. I spent the party chain smoking on the roof terrace while Farly's teenage sister, Florence, sat on my lap and showed me her yearbook. Later, when I was intoxicated, I told her

that I secretly wished one of them was unfaithful or Scott was gay, so Farly would have to return to our home. She giggled and hugged me.
'I despise that,' Farly muttered, pointing to a framed Manchester United shirt covered with the team's autographs hanging in the hall, understanding I needed something to dump my angst onto.
'Yeah, it's terrible,' I said.
'Rank,' she explained. 'I live with a boy. Urgh.'
'Girls are a lot easier to live with.'
'The very best.' She laughed. 'Do you like the apartment?'
'I adore it. I believe you'll like your time here.' And, to my chagrin, I eventually believed it.
Our undergraduate buddy Belle moved into Farly's room with a guitar and a desire to go out dancing all weekend, and things went on as usual. The refrigerator continued to leak. The basement toilet was still broken. Gordon would still come into our house uninvited on most Saturday mornings, attempting to dump horrible pieces of furniture on us as a 'gift' since he couldn't be bothered to take them to the bin. When one of us went shopping, we still did something called 'ladies' choice,' which means you receive whatever chocolate bar they came back with. I saw Farly more than I had while we were living together initially, simply because she was hyper-aware of making me feel like 'nothing' had changed. But I gradually began to see less of her. Everything shifted. Three months after they moved in together, I was sitting at my desk at work when I noticed on my phone that Scott had invited me to join a WhatsApp group called "Exciting News."
I didn't open it because I knew what it was. I'd been looking forward to this moment since Farly told me they were moving in together. I wasn't ready to know, so I kept working as if it were all a dream, an unsent note in the ether's outbox. For an hour, my phone rested on my desk, the notification gazing at me.
Finally, I received a phone call from AJ, who had also been invited to the group, and she instructed me to open it. It stated that he was suggesting. It's Valentine's Day. Four years have passed since their first date. He asked if we might gather a group of her friends and surprise her after he'd done it. I responded I'd be delighted to. I stated that I couldn't wait any longer. I stated I was overjoyed. I cried, knowing that whatever battle I was fighting with whomever I was battling had been lost.

Dilly walked by.
'Dollbird,' she called herself. 'What's the deal?'
'Nothing,' I grumbled.
'Come on,' I say. She took my hand in hers and led me to the boardroom. 'Explain what's going on.' I informed her about the proposition. She was familiar with the story, having met Farly several times and been fascinated by the Scott-Farley-Dolly love triangle for years, referring to it as "the perfect structured reality plot."
'And I know it sounds like I'm being melodramatic,' I sobbed. 'I realise people grow up and things change, but I never expected everything to alter when we were just twenty-five.' She sighed seriously and shook her head at me.
'What?' I inquired.
'I always knew we should have rigged the building with cameras when you guys moved in,' she rolled her eyes. 'I knew it; I told Dave at the time. I know you say you don't want to be on camera, but this could have been a great series arc.'
I gathered our buddies and informed them of Scott's plan. We planned a time and location where we would be waiting with a gift. I purchased them a framed print of the lyrics to 'There Is A Light That Never Goes Out,' their favourite Smiths song, from Etsy. AJ promised to get me the 'Heaven Knows I'm Miserable Now' one. I had no desire for any of this. I never wanted her to spend every weekend at barbecues in blasted Balham with Scott's friends and their wives. I didn't want to see her for dinner dates. I didn't want her to leave after only a year. I didn't want her to marry. The hardest part was that it was all my fault. If only I could turn back the clock and never set them up. I've never dated Hector. On that icy night in Notting Hill, I never returned to Hector's. I hoped I could go back in time and ignore him when he began speaking to me on the train. I wished I'd never been on that fucking train to begin with. The issue with having a Fairly in your life is that their tale feels similar to yours. She wasn't living the life I had envisioned for us, and I was lamenting the future I now knew we'd never have. We were on track until Scott: we went to the same university and opted to live in the same halls, then we lived in the same house for two years. I assumed we'd have 'The London Years' instead of 'The London Year' when we graduated. I expected to see numerous residences, not just one. I

imagined we'd spend hundreds of nights out together that would finish in the morning. I expected gigs and double dates, travels to European towns, and weeks spent stretched out on the beach side by side. I imagined we'd have a claim on each other's twenties before having to give the other one up. Scott had robbed me of our story, I felt. He'd stolen ten years from me. A month before Scott proposed, a number of us went out for drinks with Farly on a Saturday night.

'Scott mentioned something strange to me this week,' she revealed. We covertly glanced at each other with blinking, bug-wide eyes, knowing we'd already chipped in for the Smiths print and cleared Valentine's Day.

'Come on,' I urged solemnly.

'He said he had a Valentine's Day surprise for me, and it's modest yet very big. And - I know that seems strange - but a part of me wondered whether it was an engagement ring.'

'I don't think it's that,' Lacey answered abruptly, avoiding all of our concentrated stares, which would undoubtedly reveal the game.

'No, I understand. 'You're right, it won't be,' Farly answered swiftly, laughing to himself.

'Yeah,' AJ agreed. 'I think you're reading too much into that, guy.'

'But what might be modest but significant? 'I'm not sure what it is,' Farly replied.

'Oh, I'm not sure,' Lacey admitted. 'Perhaps plane tickets for a vacation or something?'

'Perhaps it's a dog collar,' I suggested bluntly.

'What?' she inquired.

'It's a modest but significant thing. Maybe he's decided to become a clergyman and wants to inform you on your anniversary.'

'Oh, Dolly, stop it,' Farly groaned.

'Or maybe... maybe,' I suggested, my mouth catching up with the litre of white wine I'd consumed. 'Perhaps he's opted to get a Manchester United face tattoo. It appears small, but it's actually quite large, isn't it? It might influence your opinion of him.' With a subtle throat-slitty move, AJ signalled me to halt. 'Or maybe it's the keys to a boat, maybe he's got a speedboat for the Thames. It's a significant lifestyle change, especially if he wants to go out on weekends. I'm sure it's expensive to keep up. Maybe that's all there is to it. He's a sailor, but he's never found the right time to tell you.'

'I don't want to guess what it is any longer,' Farly said angrily.

The night before the engagement, I couldn't sleep because I was thinking about how Farly's life was going to alter and she had no idea. 'Good luck tonight,' I texted Scott the next morning. I'm confident you'll do well. I'm hoping she says yes. If not, it's been a pleasure knowing you x.'
'Thank you for your vote of confidence, Dolls x,' he said.
We sat in the bar, waiting for Scott's text message.
'What if she says no?' AJ speculated. 'Shouldn't we just go home?'
'She won't say no,' I predicted. 'But if she does, I've already checked what else is on and there's a disco night at KOKO, so we just head there for a dance - it's ten quid on the door,' she says. Scott texted me at ten o'clock to tell us they were engaged. He'd told her they'd go out for one last celebration drink before heading home. We got a bottle of champagne, poured them two glasses, and glanced out the window while they waited for their taxi. We finally saw them go into the bar, and AJ silently gripped my sweaty palm twice, the worldwide Morse code.
'CONGRATULATIONS!' we all exclaimed as Farly entered the room. She looked at us, then at Scott, stunned. He grinned at her, and she dashed over to me for a hug.
'Congratulations,' I replied as I handed Scott his champagne glass.
'You've made my best buddy very happy,' she says.
'I'm so delighted you dated that idiot Hector,' he chuckled. 'Dolly, I adore you.'
His eyes welled up with tears, and he hugged me. I wondered if he understood how I felt. I was curious if he'd always known. Maybe that's why he sought to include me on the night they got engaged; gave me my own project; involved me in some way. Farly had asked me to be her maid of honour two hours earlier, I had consumed the lion's share of their celebratory champagne, and I was feeling loud.
'I wanna make a speech,' I said to AJ, picking up a fork to tap on my glass.
'No, sweetheart,' AJ answered, taking the fork from my hand and motioning to the other girls, who quickly removed all the cutlery from the table and handed it to the waiter. 'There will be no speeches.'
'But I'm her fucking maid of honor,' she says.
'I know, darling, but there'll be time for speeches.' I crawled beneath the table when AJ went to the bathroom and discovered her vehicle

keys in her handbag. With a ding ding ding, I clinked them on the glass.
'When I initially heard Scott and Farly were engaged - oh, sure, I was irritated,' I admitted.
'Oh my God,' Belle exclaimed.
'Because I've known this weirdo for almost fifteen years.'
'More than twenty-five years?' Lacey inquired of Hicks.
'SHUDUP!' My wine spilled onto the table as I yelled at Lacey.
'THIS IS SHIT, YOU'RE NO LONGER MAID OF HONOUR!' Farly yelled across the table, inebriated.
'But as I look about, I realise that the world is... just as it should be,' I stopped for dramatic effect. Because my dearest friend has got the title of best man.'
'Awww,' everyone exclaimed, exhaling a collective sigh of relief.
'To Scott and Farley,' I said as I sat down, tears streaming down my cheeks. Everyone applauded in a feeble manner.
'Beautiful,' Belle said quietly to me. 'I know you stole that from Julia Roberts' speech in My Best Friend's Wedding.'
'Oh, she won't know,' I said, dismissively flapping my hand.
To be honest, the rest of that evening is a bit of a haze to this day. I invited Dilly and her husband, who were in town for Valentine's Day, to join us for the festivities. I did the cancan in the bar's dining area while singing 'One' from A Chorus Line and high-kicked a tray of plates from a waiter's hands, smashing them to bits on the floor. I said my goodbyes to Scott and Farly before returning to my Camden flat and ordering everyone to keep drinking till six a.m. I awoke next to a semi-clothed Hicks with happy valentine day inscribed in liquid eyeliner over her breasts. I spent the next day on social media following Farly's 'engagement weekend' (I don't want to seem too picky about this particular detail, but I had believed one evening would suffice). Scott's buddies and their wives showered her with gifts like Smythson wedding planner notebooks and magnums of champagne, making my framed print look a little meagre. I started to feel like the fourth, forgotten Wise Man (who had brought some tat from Etsy).
'I suppose Friday night was fairly overwhelming for you,' Fairly stated over the phone. 'Are you all right?'
'I'm perfectly fine!' I'm not sure what you mean by "overwhelming". I mean, I'm not the one who proposed. You were the one who

appeared to be overwhelmed. I read on Facebook that Michelle bought you that Smythson wedding planner book - isn't that nice?'
'Do you want to go out to supper with just the two of us next week?'
'Sure.'
For the first time in four years, I emailed Hector.
Do you remember me? Scott and Farly are marrying. Thank goodness you sent me down to your kitchen naked. He responded. He'd claimed to have seen the news on Facebook. He informed me he'd abandoned the City for travel PR and had a big expense account, and he'd like to take me out for a boozy lunch to salute our matchmaking abilities. I believed we were the thin end of the matchmakers' wedge, but I said yes because I was feeling down. In a fit of forced nostalgia, I scoured my inbox for all of his previous nasty poems. I had cancelled lunch the day before.
'What made you think you'd email him?' A few days later, Farly inquired between bites of her burger at dinner.
'I'm not sure. 'I guess all I want is a boyfriend.'
'Really?' she asked as she wiped her mouth with a tissue. 'You always claim not to want one.'
'Yeah, but lately I've been feeling differently.'
'What set it off?'
What had caused it? I was envious. I wasn't jealous of Scott this time; I was jealous of Farly.
'You're getting married.'
'Why?' she inquired.
'Because I despise how different your life is today from mine. 'I hate that we used to do things at the same time and now we don't,' I grumbled. 'It bothers me that our children are so young. I despise the fact that you're preparing to buy a house with a man, and that I had to beg my landlord to let me pay my rent three weeks late this month. I despise the fact that you go about in Scott's Audi, which he got from work, while I still can't drive. I despise the fact that his pals are so dissimilar to mine, and I'm afraid they'll take you away because their lifestyles resemble your new life while mine does not. I know it seems crazy, but it's not about me ruining your good occasion, and I should just be happy for you. But I feel so far behind you, and I'm afraid you'll lose sight of me.'
'I would have found it really, extremely difficult if you had met your husband when you were twenty-two,' she remarked.

'Really?'
'Of course!' she says. I would have despised it.'
'Because I feel like I'm going insane at times.'
'You're not insane. I would have felt the same way. But I never intended to meet Scott until I was twenty-two years old. I wasn't looking for a spouse.'
'Yeah,' I admitted halfheartedly.
'And I will be there to celebrate and experience all of your life's milestones, whether they come next month or in twenty years.'
'About forty years,' I murmured. 'I still don't have curtains in my apartment.'
'We're no longer in school. Things will happen at various times. You'll be doing things ahead of me as well.'
'Like what, exactly? Meth?'
So I finally came to terms with Scott. He wasn't going away, I realised. I spent time with each of them and played the well-known and well-received role of Official Third Wheel. It's a vexing typecasting, but one I excel at. Only a few of my years on this planet have been spent in a relationship. I am The Threewheelin' Dolly Alderton, and I am well-versed and practised in third-wheeling.
I spent my entire adolescence hanging around with my pals and their boyfriends. Smiling while they battled on the sofa or pretended to play snake on my phone while they slept in a corner of the room. I'm really good at smiling and pretending with couples; it's how I spent most weekday evenings at a table in my twenties. I let them pretend to argue about who gets to load or empty the dishwasher in front of me. When they share long anecdotes about each other's sleeping habits, I chuckle along with them. I remain silent as they enthusiastically discuss details of people's lives I've never heard of ('No WAY?! Priya did not purchase those tiles! I just don't believe it! After all of this! Oh, sorry, explain to Dolly who Priya is and the entire tale of the loft conversion from beginning to end') to demonstrate that they have a tremendously exciting existence that does not involve me. And I pretend I'm not sure why I'm the third wheel; why I'm doing all the laughing and listening. But I know I'm just an aphrodisiac in their game of Domestic Bliss - I know when I leave they'll rip each other's clothes off, having gotten all worked up on an extended joint discourse about their vacation in the Philippines, especially when they both said the same island when I

asked what their favourite part was. I'm just a grudging audience member. But I continue to watch all of these shows because the alternative, losing my friends, is not an option. When Farly and Scott weren't doing Their Bit on me, I realised, much to my surprise, that Scott and I got along rather well. In fact, I resented the fact that I hadn't discovered this sooner since I would have liked his company when he came around when Farly and I were living together instead of just growling at him. He was both amusing and astute. He read the newspaper and formed thoughts. Scott turned out to be a really nice man, and it seemed apparent to me in retrospect that Farly would marry someone cool. It was something I completely misunderstood. When I wasn't busy helping Farly arrange her wedding, I was making an attempt with his pals. Whenever I'd met them before, I'd put on a tremendous, embarrassed show of proving how different I was from them. I once got exceedingly intoxicated at our house for a Sunday meal and lectured everyone on the 'meat is murder' concept while they ate their roast lamb. I once accused one of his friends of being sexist in a pub because he made a remark about my height. But after Farley and Scott got engaged, I tried everything I could to relax, be pleasant, and get to know them. After all, those were the individuals she was spending the most of her time with right now. They had to be at least half interesting. Then one Friday evening in August, we all stopped thinking about the wedding. Farly's eighteen-year-old sister Florence was diagnosed with leukaemia. 'Life is on hold,' Farly's father said in the months that followed. Life had been put on pause. The wedding date was pushed back a year. Florence was a bridesmaid, and they wanted to make sure she was healthy enough for the big day. I'd spent months worrying about the wedding, and now I couldn't care less. Farly celebrated his 27th birthday a month after his diagnosis. We wanted to celebrate with her to take her mind off Florence's condition, but she was exhausted after spending every waking hour in the hospital. She didn't want to drink, she didn't want to be in a large crowd, and she didn't want to have to tell everyone how she was doing. Her family was unable to attend because they were staying at the hospital. Scott made the decision: AJ and I would go over to their new place, and he would cook dinner for the four of us.

Farly's eleventh birthday was the first one I celebrated with her. She had more birthday candles blown out with me than without me. I recall the first one like it was yesterday, when she was just a friend I sat next to in maths class. We performed the Macarena in Bushey church hall while she wore a pink Miss Selfridge outfit.

But this was unlike any other birthday we'd ever shared. Farly was the smallest I'd ever seen her, as small and delicate as a young bird. There was no loud hugging or binge drinking. No one was more quiet and gentle than Scott.

He had gotten up early to go to the fishmonger because both AJ and I had quit eating meat. He prepared the most stunning sea bass filled with fennel and oranges with roast new potatoes, and he presented it with the bitten-tongue concentration of a MasterChef contestant. Every time he passed Farly, he kissed her on the cheek. He cradled Farly's hand beneath the table. I recognized the man she had fallen in love with.

In the kitchen, I texted Scott to let him know I had a tray of birthday cupcakes hidden behind the sofa. We waited for Farly to use the restroom, and AJ trapped her in with a chair while I frantically arranged the cakes on a dish and Scott looked for a box of matches.

'WHAT IS WRONG?!' Farly let out a yelp.

'ONLY ONE MINUTE!' As Scott and I ignited all the candles, I yelled.

We sang 'Happy Birthday' to her and gave her gifts and cards. She giggled and blew out the candles as the three of us encircled her in a large group hug.

'Why did it take so long?' she wondered. 'Did you bake those when I was pissed? I was there for so long that I started doing thigh exercises.'

'What kind of thigh exercises?' AJ inquired.

'Oh, these new lunges I've been hearing about.' She began to lean up and down, part of her old, brilliant colour dripping down her face. 'I make an effort to do them every morning. It doesn't seem to be making a difference. My legs still like massive gammon joints.' AJ began to imitate her, bobbing up and down stiff as Farly commanded her, like a Rosemary Conley film.

Scott attracted my attention as he peered across the room. He gave me a friendly smile. 'Thank you,' he said. I returned his smile and recognized the universe that now stood between us. The invisible dimension formed by our common history, affection, and future for this one individual. That's when I realised everything had changed:

we'd transitioned. We hadn't selected one another. But we were like family.

CHAPTER 8
TOTTENHAM COURT ROAD AND ORDERING SHIT OFF AMAZON

I went out to celebrate the thirtieth birthday of my friend Hannah when I was twenty-one, at the tail end of my last summer spent playing at the Edinburgh Festival before I had to go home and find a job and start an adult life. She'd been directing me in a comedy sketch production I'd been flying for, and two of the other performers and I took her out to a nice restaurant to celebrate. She had made some vague statements about dreading turning thirty in the lead-up to the day, which we all felt were overblown for humorous purposes. She set down her silverware and began crying halfway through dinner.
'Oh my goodness, Hannah, are you upset?' I inquired, now regretting the 'Happy Birthday Granny' card I had handed her.
'I'm growing old,' she admitted. 'I can sense it. I can feel it all throughout my body, and it's already slowing down. And it will just get slower.'
'You're still so young!' she said. Margaret, who was a few years her senior, said, but Hannah kept sobbing, unable to catch her breath, tears spilling into her plate. 'Do you want to go?' she asked, patting Hannah on the back. Hannah gave a nod. As we went along Princes Street, chatting about nothing, trying to keep the mood light and Hannah distracted, she came to a halt in the middle of the street and buried her face in her hands. Her tears turned into wails.
'Is this it?' she exclaimed into the dark night. 'Is this all there is to life?'
'Is that all there is to life?' Margaret asked, placing her arm around her.
'Fucking... Tottenham Court Road and ordering crap from Amazon,' she said.
Those words were stuck on the back of my mind like a Post-it note I couldn't get rid of for years. They hung there like a whispered discussion between your parents that you didn't comprehend but knew was crucial. I'd always wondered how those two precise items - Tottenham Court Road and Amazon - could bring such anguish.

'When you're not twenty-one, you'll understand,' Hannah remarked when I inquired. The year I reached twenty-five, I finally understood the machinations and subtext of that sentence. When you start to wonder if life is truly about waiting for buses on Tottenham Court Road and ordering books you'll never read from Amazon, you're experiencing an existential crisis. You are becoming aware of the banality of existence. You're now realising how meaningless everything is. You're transitioning from the realm of fantasy 'when I grow up' to the reality that you're there; it's occurring. And it wasn't what you were expecting. You are not who you expected to be. It's tough to take the day-to-day functions of life seriously once you start digging a hole with such questions. Throughout my twenty-fifth year, it was as if I had dug a trench of my own thoughts and unanswerable questions, and from there I peered up, watching people care about the things I had cared about: haircuts, the newspaper, parties, dinner, January sales on Tottenham Court Road, Amazon deals - and I couldn't imagine climbing out and knowing how to immerse myself in any of it again. I gave up alcohol for a while to try to balance my mood, but it only made me overthink even more. I experimented with Tinder dating, but the mostly platonic interactions left me feeling even more depressed and empty. My once-fervent love and attention for my profession was beginning to fade. My flatmates, AJ and Belle, frequently came into my room to find me crying while still wrapped in a towel from a three-hour shower. I found it difficult to express how I felt to others; I spent long periods of time alone. My body hummed with apathy, ennui, and worry, as low and as disruptive as a washing machine on a spin cycle that won't stop. All of this culminated in early summer when Dilly told me she believed I should quit my job to become a full-time writer, and I had no idea how to make money or where to go next. And, less than a year after Farly left, AJ revealed that she was leaving to live with her partner. I was miserable, without a job, and without a roommate. Of course, the answer is usually the same for a single twenty-something lady prone to melodrama: move to a different city. I had always loved New York and frequently visited Alex, who remained a close friend even after her brother Harry had broken our relationship years before. It felt serendipitous that she got engaged and asked me to be her bridesmaid during the summer of my discontent. Farley and I were invited to stay in their Lower East Side apartment for free while she and her fiancé were on honeymoon. We reserve our tickets, a wedding hotel, and a one-night trip to the Catskill Mountains near the conclusion of our two-week stay. It would be my and Farly's first international trip together. And it was an excellent opportunity for me to get a feel for my potential new home, including its daily operations, people, and how I might picture myself fitting in. Florence, however, was diagnosed with leukaemia just a week before our flight. Farly, understandably, felt compelled to remain at home to help her sister and family. I asked whether she needed me there as well, but she urged me to go to New York on my own and relax. I got caught in a convivial cyclone of bridesmaid obligations during my first two days in New York. Alex's whole British contingent had flown over for the wedding, and the days leading up to it were spent crafting wreaths, arranging chairs, picking up dry-cleaning, and spending time with old and familiar acquaintances. Farly was missed, but it was still the hectic, new, beautiful embrace of diversion that I craved. On the wedding day, I wore a black strappy dress with a thigh-high split (Alex encouraged this because she knew I was in desperate need of a holiday romance; I also knew I'd be seeing Harry for the first time in years) and read the poem 'The Amorous Shepherd' in the Brooklyn warehouse where they married. When I said, 'I don't regret whatever I was before because I still am; I just regret not having loved you,' I couldn't help but cry. For Alex and her husband's affection, and for the loneliness I had only recently realised I had felt for the past year. I was one of two single women at the wedding, and I considered myself fortunate to be seated next to the only single male guest: a big Welshman who constructed bridges for a job.

'Good poem,' he remarked, his voice seductive, see-sawing, sing-songy. 'The tears were a great touch,' says the author.

'It was not intended!' I exclaimed.

'That clothing surely was,' he remarked, smiling.

We drank Negroni after Negroni, ate fried chicken and mac and cheese, and flirted in a way that is only acceptable at a wedding when you're the only two single people there. We meticulously listed all of our favourite bridges in the United Kingdom. I gave him pudding with my fork. When I stood up to give my speech, he applauded and winked when I caught his eye halfway through. He acted as if he were my long-term partner. Our friendship grew with

the zeal of a foot on a pedal pressed all the way to the floor (in a way that is only appropriate when you're the only two single people at a wedding).
My Welshman left just before the first dance to take a call outdoors. Alex led her husband to the dance floor, wearing a rose crown and a long, white, kimono-sleeved gown that made her look like a Pre-Raphaelite draped in silk. The humming undulation of the most romantic music I'd ever heard performed - Phil Phillips' 'Sea Of Love' - was a real, schmaltzy, beautiful slow dance. All the other guests had joined them by the chorus, and tens of couples, including Harry and his new girlfriend, moved and smiled to the sweetly sentimental song. I sat on the porch, peering in. I tried to envision what it would be like to find security in the person you went to bed with - a concept that was completely strange to me. I pictured the spaces that lay between them, the stories they had written together, the memories and the language and the habits and the trust and the future hopes they would have talked while drinking wine late at night on the sofa. I wondered if I'd ever have that experience with someone, or if I was even designed to float in a sea of love. Whether I wanted to or not. I felt a tap on my shoulder and turned up to see another bridesmaid, Octavia. She smiled and extended her hand; she took me to the dance floor and held my hand as we danced till the song ended. After that, I went even harder on the Negronis. When I walked outside for a cigarette and ran into my Welshman, Campari gave me the confidence to push him against the brick wall and kiss him.
'I can't do that,' he murmured as he backed away.
'What's the harm?' I inquired.
'It doesn't really matter,' he grumbled. 'But I just can't do it.'
'No,' I mumbled. 'This... isn't happening like this. I'm in New York on vacation, I'm a miserable bridesmaid, and I'm wearing a slaggy dress that I paid to have taken up even higher at the dry cleaners. OK, you're my holiday fling. It has already been decided.'
'I can't,' he said. 'I wish I could, but I can't.'
'So, what was with all the -' I pretended to put pudding in his mouth. 'And the -' I said with a dramatic wink.
'I was simply... flirting,' he admitted feebly.
'Yeah, that was a complete waste of time. You know how I was seated next to an incredibly intriguing and brilliant actor? I wished I

could have had a chat with her. She appeared to be fascinating. I just said three words to her all night. I was too busy pretending to be your girlfriend.'

'Oh well, I'm sorry I was such a waste of time!' he grumbled as he returned to the party.

I went to Alex and her new husband's flat in Chinatown the next day to wish them a happy honeymoon and toast their new marriage from the roof. We caught up on wedding gossip, and they clarified the Welshman's conflicting signals (of course he had a girlfriend).

Alex showed me around the apartment and handed me the keys.

'Are you going to be alright?' she inquired.

'I'll be OK,' I assured her.

'Do you have Octavia's phone number? She'll be in town till the end of the month, so you won't be alone.'

'I'll be alright; it's excellent for me to have some alone time. Learn more about New York. It'll be a fantastic adventure.'

'Call us if you need anything,' she murmured as she hugged me.

'I most emphatically will not. 'Go to Mexico, bathe naked in the water, drink tequila, and shag yourself into oblivion,' I advised.

I awoke in the flat the next morning, fed their two black cats, watered their plants per their directions, and sat with a notepad to plan how I would spend my time here and all the things I would see and do. But there was one major issue: a magazine was paying me late for two pieces of work totaling just under a thousand pounds, which I had budgeted to be more than enough for my New York expenses. I had £34 in my bank account and eleven days in New York left. As a freelance journalist, I was frequently chasing accounts departments for money three months after an article was published and the invoice was filed. But it had never been more critical. I called my editor, who directed me to the accounts department, which passed me from person to person, attempting to figure out where my late money was. I lie on Alex's bed for an hour with my phone on loudspeaker, the tinny hold music blasting, the long-distance phone call eating up my bill minute by minute. I was told that I will be paid 'soon' by the individual I spoke with. With no money and no friends, it became clear that New York was a totally different place than the previous times I had visited Alex on vacation. It's a bad place to be broke. In contrast to London, all museums and galleries demand a public admission fee, the majority of which are $25, which would have depleted my remaining finances. It was also the middle of August, so it was oppressively hot, limiting the amount of time I could spend wandering around or sitting in the park. The city I had always loved, where I had always felt welcome, seemed to want me to leave. When I was walking down Fifth Avenue, I looked up at the skyscrapers and imagined them to be big, terrible, towering monsters chasing me to JFK airport. I started to notice all the little things about New York that irritated me previously. I discovered how inefficient and perplexing the subway system was. Unlike the London Underground, which has a colourful and sometimes regal array of line names (Jubilee, Victoria, Piccadilly), the lines all have the most indistinguishable and uninspired names possible (A, B, C, 1, 2, 3, etc.). thus B can easily sound like D, thus 1 is most likely 3. It's impossible to remember which letter or number you're supposed to catch if you don't write it down. Trains only come every 10 minutes in many stations, so if you're doing three changes and you're unlucky with timings, this might mean an extra half-hour of standing around on blistering hot platforms. To make matters worse, the majority of platforms lack information boards indicating when the next train is scheduled to arrive. Then there were the 'ball-busters' of New York, those noisy, demanding folks who snap at you in shops, cafes, and lines. The ones that are either really unpleasant or want to provide you with "the full immersive New York experience." Perhaps I found it amusing when I was feeling secure and joyful. But now that I was feeling so alone, I despised how much I was being yelled at. 'HEY, LADY - GET OUT OF THE FRICKIN' WAY!' yelled a passing waiter as I stood at the counter to get a bagel at Katz's Deli. In New York, I also observed how much I was shoved. The place's collective ambition had never felt so daunting. Everyone was focused on their own task, and no one looked at each other. People strolled with their arms swinging like they were marching, shouting into their hands-free. Even their relationship was ambitious; I spent a day in a cafe overhearing two female friends babbling at one other about how they were going to meet guys, and they made it sound like a military operation - it was all dates, numbers, arithmetic, and rules. And the rules, Christ. I had never realised how preoccupied they were with rules. I was chastised for picking up and smelling an orange at a supermarket before purchasing it. When I went to Apthorp (Nora Ephron's cherished

apartment complex about which she wrote an essay), I was told off for getting too close to the beautiful fountain in the courtyard. I had never considered myself to be a particularly anarchic creature, but New York's disciplinarians brought it out in me. Then there were the apathetic hipsters. individuals who gave you fine coffee or worked in interesting stores; individuals who, instead of smiling, remarked plainly, 'That's the funniest thing I've ever heard in my entire life,' with a straight, expressionless face when someone told them a joke. The ones who stared at you for longer than you felt comfortable with. All the attitude of a Hackney twat, none of the self-awareness, humour, or cynicism. Scenesters under thirty in New York are some of the coldest, most uninviting people I've ever met. After a week in New York, I discovered that places are kingdoms of memories and relationships, and that the landscape is only ever a reflection of how you feel on the inside. I felt more empty, exhausted, and depressed there than I did at home. The desire to relocate decreased with each passing day. I had the unsettling realisation that 'Tottenham Court Road and Amazon' would accompany me wherever I went - I was still the same unfulfilled person on vacation as I was at home. I thought I was booking a trip out of my head when I booked the flights, but I wasn't. The scenery had changed, but my psychological state had not: I was worried, restless, and self-loathing. I spent the evening trying 'Tinder tourism' as a way of meeting new people as I laid on Alex's sofa, working my way through a bottle of leftover wedding Prosecco that she had told me to help myself to. Almost everyone was right-swiped by me. I sent a vague, cheerful broadcast message to all of my matches, introducing myself as a "visitor from London" searching for some New Yorkers to "show her a good time." At midnight, I opened a second bottle of Prosecco, just in time to receive a video call from AJ and India.
'Heeeeeeeey!' they all exclaimed from around my kitchen table.
'Hello, guys!' I exclaimed. 'Are you mad?'
'Yeah,' India replied. 'We just bought three bottles of wine at the Nisa Local.'
'Good. 'I'm also irritated.'
AJ asked, staring into the camera, "Who are you with?" I considered informing them about my bad luck, but I didn't want to worry them. More significantly, my pride would not permit it. I had been giving

the idea on all social media platforms that I was having the trip of a lifetime.

'No one,' I said. 'I'm taking it easy tonight.'

We caught up for fifteen minutes, and I was glad to see their familiar faces and hear all about their adventures.

'Are you alright?' AJ inquired as to when I said good-by. 'You appear to be depressed.'

'I'm OK,' I replied. 'I'm missing you both.'

'We miss you, too!' she exclaimed. They both blew kisses at me before leaving me alone.

I was halfway through my second bottle of Prosecco when I received a message from one of my Tinder matches, Jean, a thirty-two-year-old French stockbroker who asked if I wanted to go out for a late drink. This man would be my holiday fling; just the kind of fun, empowering adventure I needed to turn this trip into an adventure and make me feel like my old self again. But he lived in SoHo, a mile away, which I couldn't walk because a thunderstorm had started outside and I didn't have enough money in my account for a taxi.

'I have money,' he wrote. 'I'll cover the cost of your taxi.' I decided to disregard the Pretty Woman subtext of this offer, put on makeup and heels, and stand in the rain for a passing cab. A mix of torrential rain and torrential alcohol forced my phone to slide from my grasp when I hailed one. The screen shattered into a thousand pieces, raindrops flowed into the cracks, and the screen faded to dark. He was, thankfully, standing outside when I arrived at the address he'd given me. He paid for the cab and opened the door for me to exit.

'Thank you for coming,' he said, drawing my face in for a kiss. For a brief moment, this complete stranger's attention filled me with a little fizz of joy, and the gravity of my deep-rooted despair felt like it had fled the building. Then I realised how pathetic and telling this was, and I became even more depressed. I needed another beverage. Jean was pleasant enough. We had nothing in common, but the beer he offered me and the packet of Lucky Strike we chain-smoked on his sofa kept the talk flowing. I had the impression he did this frequently. He took me to his bedroom after an hour of chatting and snogging. A stark white box with odd neon lights on the floor in place of a bed. As we undressed each other, I attempted to ignore the setting. He said, 'Wait, wait,' as I unbuttoned his jeans. 'I exclusively do group sex,' she says.

'What does that even mean?' I mumbled.
'I can only have sex if someone is watching,' he said as if it were obvious. 'Or if someone decides to join us.'
'All right,' I said. 'Well, that's not going to happen any time soon, so-'
'My flatmate lives next door,' he explained. 'He wishes to enter. I'll tell him it's fine.'
'No, it's not OK,' I answered, immediately realising that this was not going to be a major adventure. I was in a bedroom with a man who resembled Patrick Bateman. 'I don't want to do that,' I muttered, scared, hearing my heartbeat in my eardrums and searching for the nearest window. 'Come on, it'll be great,' he urged as he tried to kiss me. 'You appeared to be a party girl.'
'No, I'm not, and I don't want to.'
'OK, so that's something we don't do.' He rolled over and shrugged.
I realised how stupid I had been, how irresponsible I had been in my hunt for a distraction from myself. I was intoxicated and alone in a strange city; no one knew where I was; I had no money and no phone.
'I believe I'll walk home,' I remarked as I got out of his bed.
'OK,' he said. 'It is, however, raining. You are welcome to stay here.'
I looked at his watch; it was four a.m. I could sleep until the storm passed and it was light outside, then try to find my way back to Alex's place. I slept as far away from him as I could, pressing my face against his white wall. I awoke at half past seven, dressed, and walked into the living room to retrieve my bag. An extremely angry-looking man in a navy dressing robe sat on the sofa. Four electric fans that hadn't been there the night before had appeared, and all of the windows were open. Sticked to the wall were scraps of paper with FUMER TUE scrawled in red pen and SMOKING KILLS written underneath.
'Good morning!' I said, a little uncomfortably.
'Get. The ferk. 'Get out of my place,' he said, his French accent stronger than Jean's.
'Can I apologise?'
'I suffer from asthma. Are you aware of this? I suffer from severe asthma. So, why are you in my apartment at three a.m. chain smoking your awful cigarettes?'
'I'm very sorry, Jean said it was fi-fi-fi-fi-fi-fi-fi-
'Jean, go ferk 'imself,' he snarled.

I returned to Jean's room.
'Hey,' I said as I shook him awake. 'Hey, your flatmate is in there, and he's going crazy.'
Jean blinked open his eyes and glanced at his watch.
'I'm late for work!' he exclaimed accusingly.
'He's going insane in there,' I said. 'He's upset because we smoked last night. He's got all of these admirers and all of these signs. It's a little...' 'The Rain Man.'
'He's unhappy because you wouldn't have sex with him, not because we were smoking.'
'OK, I'll go,' I said. 'Have a nice life.' I strolled out of the flat, humbly nodding at my enraged French housemate.
'GET OUT. GET OUT. GET OUT. 'GET ZE FERK OUT, YOU LITTLE BEETCH!' he yelled.
I teetered into the brilliant SoHo sunlight, feeling sick to my stomach. I went to the nearest ATM to withdraw ten dollars but was told I didn't have enough money. A wave of nausea washed over me, and I realised I hadn't eaten in two days. As I tried to find my way home, I stopped into Starbucks, hoping for milk jugs near the sugar sachets. I requested a paper cup from the man behind the counter and filled it with milk, sipping it carefully as I sat at a table.
'Are you okay, honey?' said a middle-aged woman. 'You have the appearance of...' She looked over my clothes, my eyes coated with mascara dust from the night before, and the cup of milk in my hand.
'Like a stray kitten,' she says.
'I'm fine,' I said. I'm feeling worse than ever.
I walked in circles for a couple of hours till I came upon a block of flats I recognized. I arrived at Alex's apartment, stuffed my phone in rice, and cuddled up with her cats beneath the blanket, wishing I could pull the duvet up over the trip as well. But I couldn't even afford a sandwich, let alone a trip home so early. And I'm not sure I wanted to go home - I was stuck between two cities I didn't want to be in. I couldn't call Farley and ask for aid because she needed it considerably more than I did. I couldn't call my parents because I couldn't stand worrying them, and I was ten years too old to be bailed out of anything. I eventually called Octavia, who was quite helpful. She took me out for dim sum, held my hand as I chatted, hugged me, and lent me money. The next day, I took a three-hour coach ride to a little village in upstate New York's Catskills. Farly and I had already

paid for the cabin, so I figured I'd utilise it, and I was grateful for the opportunity for some space, quiet, and open skies. I arrived in the middle of the morning, dumped my baggage, and went for a long stroll to clear my mind. I was already feeling better by the time I got back to my cabin in the afternoon, having marvelled at the vastness of the mountains and considering the notion of starting over when I got home. I went into town in the evening and ate cheese fries at a local diner. The sound of crickets and the friendliness and chit-chat of the locals pleased me. When I returned, there was a bonfire burning behind my cabin, so I took one of my blankets from my room and sat next to it, gazing up at the stars. I breathed for what felt like the first time since arriving in New York. When I returned to my bed, I found a fresh Tinder message - a late response to the 'come one, come all' blanket message I had drunkenly sent two nights before. Adam was his name. He was twenty-six years old, with a great all-American smile, Brooklyn beard, and man bun. 'Hello, lady,' he wrote. 'I'm sorry for not responding sooner - how are you?'
'I wish you had responded sooner,' I lamented. 'I could have ended up on a date with you instead of being forced into a threesome with two Frenchmen,' she says.
'Oh boy,' he exclaimed. 'New York may be challenging. 'How are things going for you?'
'I despise it,' I admitted. 'I'm in the Catskills for the night, and it's a much-needed respite.'
'How long do you plan to stay in town before returning home?'
'Three exhausting days. 'I return early tomorrow evening.'
'When you go back, come hang out with me,' he added. 'I swear I won't try to have a threesome with you. If you want, I can just be your friend.'
A companion. Perhaps I needed a new pal. After another lengthy hike and a swim, I caught a late-afternoon bus back to Manhattan, took the subway to Brooklyn, and arrived at Adam's door.
'Hey,' he said as he emerged from the front door, his blue eyes shining behind horn-rimmed glasses, his arms outstretched for a hug. 'It's a pleasure to meet you. Welcome return to the city you despise.'
'Thank you,' I replied, slipping into his embrace and savouring the fresh, soapy scent of his flannel shirt.
'I'll make you fall in love with it.'

Adam showed me around his apartment and we drank some wine. We talked for hours, telling each other stories about our favourite music, movies, friends and families, and careers. He was sincere, bright-eyed, bushy-tailed, and inquisitive; he was precisely what I needed. We were kissing by the middle of the evening. I was laying in his bed by midnight, my face pushed up against his. It was this man's warm touch, his kind heart, and the tenderness he showed me that made me open up. So I told him everything; I gave everything up for free. I informed him about my early twenties' heartbreak. I told him about how I had spent years starving myself in an attempt to acquire control. I told him about the one time I'd been in love; the intimacy I couldn't stand, the reliance I despised. I told him how, one by one, my pals had fallen in love and abandoned me. I told him how my anxiety had creeped up on me in catatonic flare-ups since I was a child, and how I couldn't stand near windows because I was constantly afraid of plummeting to my death. I told him about my best friend's little sister, with whom I grew up, who was in the hospital with cancer. I told him that I felt I was in over my head with maturity and that I couldn't call anyone for help. I told him how easily I buried difficulties beneath a tangle of distractions. I could only relate these things in an ephemeral realm of fiction where I had no accountability; I only had the correct vocabulary for my anguish with a stranger.
'You're so sad,' he stroked my cheek. To stop the tears, I closed my eyes.
'I'm really lost,' I admitted.
'You're not lost anymore,' he whispered as he drew me closer to him. And I wanted to trust him, so I did for the time being.
'I want to say something, but it doesn't make sense,' he muttered as he kissed my head.
'What?'
'I adore you,' he said, sighing. 'And I don't want you to think I'm dangerous or nuts like that insane French guy, which I know I can't be because I've known you for -' He looked at his watch and saw that it was six hours. But I think I might like you. 'Fuck it, I love you already.' 'I love you, too,' I said to myself. I realised how ridiculous my statements were the moment they left my mouth. But I knew I wasn't speaking to him; I was speaking to something else. To the belief in goodness and hope. Adam took the next day off from work,

his first sick day in his life, and showed me around parts of town I'd never seen before. We walked, spoke, ate, drank, and kissed. In two days, we had a typical vacation romance - we couldn't remember what life was like without each other, but we knew we'd never live life without each other. I stayed with him the next night. The next day, I had to drag myself away from Adam for three hours to see Octavia, who couldn't believe what had happened since I last saw her. We climbed to the top of 30 Rock and gazed out over the gorgeous, merciless city. 'I guess I want to go home,' I remarked as I looked out at the lights dancing off the Hudson River.

On my last day, Adam drove me to JFK. He grabbed my shoulders and stared at me after a long goodbye kiss.

'OK, I've got this notion,' he continued.

'What?'

'Don't think I'm crazy.'

'OK.'

'Stay,' he advised.

'I'm sorry, but I can't stay.'

'What's the harm? You're unhappy at home. You despise London. You are unemployed. You have no idea what you want to do next. Stay here and restart.'

'How would I live?' I wondered.

'With me,' he replied.

'How am I going to pay my rent?'

'We'll work it out,' he assured her. 'You'll be able to find a job and write all you've ever wanted to write. I'll offer you your own personal space and time. Consider how much more liberated you'll feel here.'

'What if your ironclad immigration system tries to deport me?'

'Then I'm going to fucking marry you,' he added. 'Do you want to hear that? Because I'm going to do it. I'll take you down to City Hall first thing tomorrow morning and marry you to the death. Then you're free to stay for as long as you wish.'

'I can't do it,' I explained. 'It's just absurd,' says the author.

'How come you won't stay?' he asked, gently leaning his head against mine. 'You were the one who stated you had nothing at home waiting for you.'

I pondered for a time.

'Because I'm the issue,' I explained. 'It's not the city. None of the circumstances are the issue. I'm the one who needs to change.' There was silence between us. Then we kissed for the final time. 'Call me when you land,' he instructed. 'And don't get drunk on the plane; the plane won't crash.' On the way home, I fantasised about Tottenham Court Road and bought crap from Amazon. When I hugged my mother, I remembered Farly's laugh, the sound of my flatmates getting ready for work in the morning, and the fragrance of my mother's perfume in her hair. I reflected on the wonderful mundanity of life and how fortunate I was to be living it. It was the day before my 26th birthday. When I got home, Belle and AJ were at work, but there was a weird homemade cake and a banner wishing me a happy birthday. We all went out dancing in Camden the next evening to celebrate, and I told them about my unusual two weeks away. Lauren and I sat up drinking and playing guitar until the early hours of the next morning, when Adam delivered a large bouquet of red roses. Things improved for a while when I returned home. The heavy cloak of grief that had enveloped me for so long began to lift. I devised a proper strategy for what I intended to accomplish next. I fell in love with my city all over again. I ate Toffee Crisps and read Bill Bryson's books about England. I remembered how fortunate I was to live in the neighbourhood where I had grown up, surrounded by my friends. I quit my job and went freelancing two months after I returned. A month later, I was offered a piece in The Sunday Times. Lauren and I created a short film about a twenty-five-year-old woman who has no idea who she is and seeks for solutions other than within herself. AJ moved out, and India, another great university acquaintance, stepped in. We left Camden's old yellow palace and relocated two miles north to a flat with no mice, a working toilet, and central heating. My saviour, Octavia, returned to London and became a dear friend. Adam and I have always maintained in touch and will continue to do so; he visits me in London and I always have lunch with him when I'm in New York. He reminds me of a turbulent period in my life, the stories of which I enjoy remembering but never want to relive. When I was twenty-five and feeling rootless and lost, I almost moved across the nation for a man I didn't know. He's got his half of the story, and I've got mine; we wear them about like those cheesy teenage heart necklaces.

CHAPTER 9
MY THERAPIST SAYS

'What brings you here?'
What was I doing there? I never expected to be there. Just beyond Oxford Circus, in a modest room with cream carpets and a burgundy sofa. Where, no matter how hard I inhaled when I came in, it always smelled like molecular perfume and nothing else - no leftover lunch, no cooling coffee, no trace of a life outside this room other than this woman's perfume. When I caught a whiff of it on a woman at a party, it made my heart drop and reminded me of one p.m. on a Friday afternoon. I was there for an hourly fee. A commentator's box, the TV studio of post-match analysis, existed in a vacuum of life where nothing existed but discussion between two people. The less popular debate show that airs alongside the main event. This was the case. It takes two to tango. This was Defrosted Dancing on Ice. This was the place I would always think of when I was about to make a stupid mistake; in a pub's toilet, with a man in the back of a taxi. This was the chamber that promised to change my life. I had always promised myself that I would never be in a situation like this. But I had no idea where else to go but there. I'd exhausted all other possibilities. I was twenty-seven years old and I felt like I was about to collapse from a storm of anxiety. I'd been freelancing for nine months and had spent practically every day alone with my thoughts. I had pushed away my friends' and family's concerns; I was often on the point of tears, but I couldn't talk to anyone. Every morning, I awoke with no idea where I was or what was going on; I returned to my life as if the previous night's sleep had been a punch in the head that had left me bloodied. I was there because I had no choice. I went because I had put it off; because I always stated I didn't have any money or time; because it was frivolous and ridiculous. I told a buddy I felt like I was about to implode, and she offered me a woman's phone number to contact. I'd run out of reasons.
'I'm afraid I'm going to fall and die,' I said. Eleanor peeked over her spectacles, then returned to her page, furiously jotting notes. She had black, semi-parted, flicky fringe in the manner of the 1970s, brown, feline eyes, and a powerful nose. She had to be in her early forties. She reminded me of a younger Lauren Hutton. I saw her arms were muscular, tanned, and lovely. I assumed she thought I was a pathetic crybaby. A massive loser. An overprivileged girl squandering all her hard-earned money so she could blab about herself for an hour once

a week. She undoubtedly spotted women like me approaching from a long distance away.

'I can't open or close any windows in my flat; I have to ask someone else to do it,' I said, clipped and quiet to keep tears at bay, which felt like they were pressing up against the back wall of my eyeballs like water to a flood barrier. 'Sometimes I can't even enter a room if a window is open because I'm afraid of falling out. And when a train draws into a tube station from the tunnel, I have to stand with my back to the wall. I imagine myself collapsing in front of it and dying. Every time I blink, I notice it. Then I'll spend the entire night replaying it in my thoughts, and I won't be able to sleep.'

'Right,' she said, her voice thick with an Australian accent. 'And how long have you felt this way?'

'It's been pretty awful in the last six months,' I explained. 'But it's been on and off for the better part of ten years. When I'm stressed, I drink excessively. The death obsession is similar. The obsession with the flavour of the month is waning.'

I walked her through The Best of My Recurrent Emotional Turmoil. I discussed my weight, which had fluctuated as much as cloud formations, and how I could look at every photo of myself taken since 2009 and tell her exactly how much I weighed in each one. I told her about my unquenchable thirst when most people my age now knew when to stop, how I'd always been known for knocking it back at record speed, the vast black holes in my memory from these nights over the years, my increasing shame and distress over these last hours, and that unrecognisable madwoman running around town for whom I was supposed to be responsible, but who I had no recollection of being or knowing. I told her about my unwillingness to commit to a relationship, my desire with male attention, and my concurrent dread of becoming really close to someone. How tough it had been for me to watch all of my friends, one by one, ease into long-term relationships as if they were lowering themselves into a cool swimming pool on a hot day. Every partner I'd had had wondered why I couldn't do the same, and I'd always worried that I was romantically wired incorrectly. We discussed how I had spread myself like the final spoonful of Marmite across as many lives as possible. I informed her that I had given practically all of my energy to others when no one had asked for it. I expressed how I thought this gave me control over what other people thought of me, but it made me feel more and more like a fraud. I told her how I fantasised about what people said behind my back about me, and how I would probably agree with practically any insult thrown at me anyhow. I told her about the lengths I'd gone to get approval: spending all of my money on rounds of drinks for people I'd never met and not being able to pay my rent the following week; starting Saturday nights at four p.m. and ending them at four a.m. to attend six separate birthday parties for people I hardly knew. This had made me feel exhausted, heavy, spineless, and self-loathing. The tragic irony was that I had the best friends in the world, yet I couldn't tell them anything. How deeply ingrained my fear of dependence was. That I could cry in the bed of a stranger I met in New York but couldn't seek support from my greatest friends.

'But none of this is having any noticeable impact on my life,' I pointed out. 'I feel stupid for being here since it might all be so much worse. I have wonderful friends and a wonderful family. My work is progressing nicely. From the outside, no one would notice anything wrong with me. I'm just feeling crappy. Every time.'

'If you're feeling awful all the time,' she explained, 'it's having a very, very huge effect on your life.'

'I suppose.'

'You feel like you're about to fall because you've been divided up into a hundred different floating parts,' she explained. 'You're all over the place,' she says. You have no desire to root. You have no idea how to be yourself.' My eyeballs' back wall eventually gave way, and tears streamed from the deepest well in the pit of my stomach.

I told her, 'I feel like nothing is keeping me together any longer,' my breathlessness punctuating my phrases like hiccups, the torrent of tears on my cheeks as hot and free-flowing as blood.

'Of course you do,' she responded, her voice softening. 'You have no feeling of self.'

That is why I was present. The light bulb went off. I thought I was afraid of falling, but the truth was that I didn't know who I was. And the things I tried to fill that void no longer worked; they just made me feel even further alienated from myself. This enormous anxiety had been in the mail for quite some time and had finally arrived, fluttered through the postal box, and dropped at my feet. This diagnosis astonished me since I thought my sense of self was rock solid. This is what Generation Sense of Self does. Since 2006, we have been filling out 'About Me' sections. I believed I was the most sensitive selfie-taker I knew.

'You will never know what I truly think of you,' she stated as I was about to depart, letting me know she had already picked up on my working style. 'You might be able to tell if I like you by my demeanour, but you'll never know what I think of you on a personal level. If we want to make any progress, you must get rid of that thought.'

I felt an uneasy paranoia at first, followed by an almost immediate sense of absolute relief. She was instructing me not to make stupid jokes. She was ordering me to stop apologising for consuming her Kleenex supply on the table next to me. She was telling me that in this room, I wouldn't have to labour over every word, gesture, and anecdote in the hope that she would like me. This lady, with no sense of self, self-regard, or self-esteem - a shapeshifting, people-pleasing presence; a twisted knot of anxiety - was being allowed to just be. She was telling me that in this room right beyond Oxford Circus, with the cream carpet and the burgundy sofa, I was safe to let go.

I walked the five and a half miles home from her office. I was both relieved that I had finally found my way to that chamber and oppressed by the weight of what was to come. I convinced myself that everything will be resolved in three months.

'She thinks I have no self-esteem,' I informed India as she prepared our dinner that night.

'That's rubbish,' she retorted angrily. 'You have a better sense of self than anyone I've ever met.'

'Yeah, but not that type of self-esteem,' I replied. 'Not, for example, how I intend to vote in the EU referendum or what my favourite manner to serve potatoes is. She implies that instead of being entire, I cut myself up into different pieces to distribute to different people. I'm agitated and unsettled. I don't know what I'd do without all the things that keep me going.'

'I had no idea you felt this way.'

'I feel like I'm crumbling,' I admitted.

'I don't want you to be unhappy,' India whispered, holding me barefoot in our kitchen while the spaghetti bubbled gently on the stove. 'I don't want you to do this if it will make you unhappy.'

The next Friday, I informed Eleanor that India had told her she didn't want me to go through this because she was afraid it would make me sad. I assured her I was only half-joking.

'OK, well, news flash,' she screamed in her reassuringly straightforward, sarcastic tone that I would grow to crave throughout the year. 'You're already depressed. You're so depressing.'

'I know, I know,' I said, reaching for another Kleenex. 'I apologise for utilising all of these. I'm sure you will get a lot done in your area of work.' She told me that was exactly why they were there. So the procedure began. Every week, I went in and we conducted detective work on myself to figure out how I became who I was after twenty-seven years. We conducted a forensic examination of my past, sometimes discussing events from the previous night, sometimes events from a PE class twenty years ago. Therapy is like excavating your psyche until you find something useful. It's a personal weekly episode of Time Team, produced by the therapist, Mick Aston, and the patient, Tony Robinson. We discussed and talked until she proposed a cause-and-effect hypothesis that fit, and then we figured out how to improve it. She would assign me chores such as things to try, things to work on, questions to answer, thoughts to ponder, and discussions to have. I sobbed every Friday afternoon for two months. I slept for eleven hours every Friday night. The common misconception about therapy is that it is all about blaming others; nevertheless, as the weeks progressed, I discovered the reverse to be true. I'd heard of therapists who played a defensive, deluded mum role in their patients' lives, always assuring them that it wasn't their fault, but the fault of the lover, boss, or best friend. Eleanor never allowed me to shift the blame to someone else and constantly made me rethink what I had done to end up in such a poor situation, which is why I dreaded our sessions. 'Unless someone dies,' she said one Friday, 'if something awful happens in a relationship, you have had a part in it.'

After a few months, Eleanor and I actually laughed together for the first time. After a stressful work week, I arrived in a wreck. I was short on money and self-esteem, anxious about paying my rent, and concerned that my job was going nowhere. My paranoia was out of control; I had convinced myself that everyone I had ever worked for thought I was inept, untalented, and useless. For three days, I didn't leave the apartment. I told her about a vivid nightmare in which a boardroom full of people I didn't know said I was a lousy, incapable writer. She gazed at me as I spoke, then her expression scrunched in surprise.

'I mean, I think it's absurd that you think that,' she exhaled and raised her eyebrows. The rougher she was, the more widely, brashly Australian she became. I looked up from my tissue, which was not the reaction I had hoped for.

'Whole boardrooms of people you've never met?' she exclaimed, shaking her head. 'That is EXTREMELY narcissistic.'

'Well,' I responded, snorting with laughter. 'Yeah. When you put it that way. 'It's absurd.'

'No one is mentioning you.'

'Yeah,' I murmured, patting my tears with a tissue, suddenly feeling like a Woody Allen character. 'You are correct.'

'Seriously!' she exclaimed, her fringe flicking away from her high cheeks. 'You're not particularly intriguing, Dolly.'

I had my first tear-free session when I was in my third month. The Kleenex box remained unopened. A significant step forward in therapy. While my closest friends supported the process, it soon became clear that self-examination rendered me dull to the wrong people. I began to drink less and less, always wondering if I was doing it for enjoyment or to distract myself from a problem. I tried to quit pleasing people-pleasing, knowing that freely giving my time and energy was what was chipping away at the gap that I didn't want to turn into a quarry. I was more honest; I informed people when I was irritated, insulted, or angry, and I cherished the sense of calm that came with integrity, even if it came at the expense of an awkward conversation. As I grew more self-aware, I unavoidably made a fool of myself for the pleasure of others significantly less. I felt like I was expanding week by week, as if my insides were photosynthesizing with each new behaviour I implemented. I acquired a verdant sad fixation with indoor plants. I researched what plants to put in every nook and cranny of light and shadow, and I filled my apartment with an abundance of green; pothos plants slid down bookcases, a Boston fern stood on top of my fridge, and a Swiss cheese plant fanned against my brilliant, white bedroom wall. I hung a flawless philodendron over my bed, and every night, a cool droplet fell off the heart-shaped apex of its leaves and onto my head. India and Belle questioned my health, comparing it to Chinese water torture. But I'd heard that it was guttation, a process in which a plant sheds excess water at night; it works hard to get rid of everything, placing strain on its roots. And I told them that meant a lot to me. I was doing something with the philodendron.

'Any more plants in here,' Farly said one day as he surveyed my chamber, 'and it'll turn like Little Shop of Horrors.'

When I didn't drink as much, I had the novel experience of waking up with a linear remembrance of the night. The things people said; the way they looked; the signals they believed were subtle between them. When I showed up to a social event, I realised that everyone wanted the bad stuff. They wanted another bottle of wine, they wanted to phone a drug dealer, they wanted to sit outside and chain-smoke, they wanted to drunkenly chat about someone we knew. On a night out, I had unknowingly become a black-market trader. I was everyone's go-to person for bad behaviour, and I didn't realise it until I stopped.

Eleanor's most vicious and brilliant takedown came as we were discussing this one Friday afternoon.

'I've concluded that people want me to chatter,' I informed her. 'It's what they anticipate of me when I go somewhere, especially if they're in trouble.'

'Did you gossip, too?'

'A little,' I admitted. 'I had no idea how much I used to do it.'

'What made you do it?'

'I'm not sure. To feel close to others? To strike up a conversation? 'Perhaps to feel powerful,' I reasoned. 'It's only for that reason that people gossip. 'I clearly did it to feel powerful.'

'Yes, you did,' she responded with a small smile reserved for when she was relieved I arrived before her. 'It's putting down other people so you can feel big.'

'I suppose it is,' says the speaker.

'Do you know anyone else who does that?' There was a brief pause. 'Donald Trump,' he says. I couldn't stop giggling.

'Eleanor. 'I've grown to enjoy your kind of rough love,' I told her. 'But even for you, that's a bit much.'

'Fine, Nigel Farage then,' she remarked, slightly shrugging as if I were being picky.

As I stepped out into Regent Street, I texted Farly, "My therapist compared me to Donald Trump today." 'I believe I'm making good progress.'

Then, about five months into therapy, I felt as if we'd hit a brick wall. My growth has stalled. With her, I found myself being protective. She said I was acting protective around her. In one session, I offered that there might not be an answer in dissecting my life's events and decisions; in going over and over what occurred with that lover once or what my parents said or didn't say when I was growing up. That it was all a waste of time; that I was just born this way. Did she think it was possible that I was born this way? She gave me a blank stare.

'No, I don't,' she answered.

'Well, obviously you don't,' I responded sarcastically. 'Because there would be no need for your employment otherwise.'

If I messed up that week, I'd plan out the story I'd tell her so she'd be kind with me. Then I realised how much I was spending to see her; all the additional work I'd had to do to make ends meet; what a pleasure it was to be able to afford it at all. And what a colossal waste of money that would have been if I hadn't told her the truth. I chatted with other analysis buddies who stated they were apprehensive before their sessions because they were trying to think of something tasty to tell the therapist. I felt just the opposite. I was continually thinking about what I could withhold from her or what positive spin I could put on a tale to make it appear less horrible than it really was. But, of course, she was always able to see straight through it. Because I'd told her how I worked. And I always despised how well she knew me, and whenever she challenged me, I fell into tears. I didn't dislike her for questioning what I'd done; I disliked myself for doing it in the first place. At six months, I almost said, "Well, what makes YOU so fucking wise about all this stuff?" Come on, people. In a session, tell me how beautiful YOU are. I realised I needed to take a vacation from it, but I didn't tell her. She said she sensed some anger from me, but I told her I was alright. I began cancelling sessions. I was absent for a month and a half. When I saw her again, she was significantly more understanding than I remembered, and I wondered if I had invented her tenacious and relentless line of questioning. Perhaps she had become the blank canvas on which I hurled all my rage and condemnation at myself. In the middle of our hour together, she inquired why I'd stopped visiting regularly without telling her. I considered fabricating an explanation; I considered the money and time I was investing in this; and how it was too late to back out now.

'I'm not sure,' I admitted.

'Is it because it's all getting too personal?' she inquired. 'Is this a dependency problem? You don't want to rely on it?'

'Yeah,' I admitted, sighing. 'I think that's it; I think I wanted to be in charge of it.'

'Yeah, I guess that might be it,' she thought aloud. 'Whatever is going on in your life outside of here is reflected in here.'

'I get what you mean.'

'What do you want to control?'

'Everything,' I realised as I said it out loud. 'I'm attempting to influence everyone's perception of me. Everyone's attitude toward me. I'm attempting to prevent negative things from happening. Death, calamity, and disappointment are all possibilities. I'm trying to keep everything under control.'

Her enlightenment became my epiphany, and I resolved to surrender to the process. With trust, I surrendered myself up to Eleanor and began a new cycle of our time together.

'You have to keep coming here, and we have to keep talking,' she said. 'We need to talk and talk and discuss until we can connect everything.'

I suppose part of the issue was that I couldn't handle the fact that Eleanor knew so much about me - the darkest caverns of who I am, my most sacred, embarrassing, humiliating, dreadful, beautiful memories. And I received no information about her in return. Sometimes I envisioned Eleanor at home, wondering what her life would be like if she wasn't a therapist. I wondered what she told her friends about me, whether she ever read my articles, checked my social media feeds, or googled me like I did the first time I received an invoice with her complete name on it. A few weeks later, she inquired about my therapy experience, and I expressed my dissatisfaction with not knowing anything about her. I informed her that while I recognized that this was the proper exchange, I felt it was sometimes unjust. Why did I have to be naked every week when she was always fully clothed?

'What do you mean, you don't know anything about me?' she inquired, perplexed.

'I'm not familiar with you as a person.'
'You do,' she confirmed.
'No, I don't; I couldn't tell a single one of my friends anything about you.'
'Every week, you come in here and we chat about love, sex, family, friendship, happiness, and sadness. You already know what I think about all of this.'
'However, I don't know if you're married, if you have children, or where you reside. I'm not sure where you go out. 'I'm not sure if you go to the gym,' I added, thinking mainly of her toned arms, which I usually found myself glancing at in particularly trying moments, wondering what weights she used.
'Do you think knowing any of that will help you grasp who I am?' she inquired. 'You seem to know a lot about me.'
I eventually learned the Eleanor language. She usually emphasised, after a particularly tearful session, 'Take good care' - emphasis on the 'good'. 'Don't get completely leathered this weekend,' he said. It was also horrible when she said 'Oh boy' after I told her something. The worst was, by far, 'I've been worrying about you this week.' When Eleanor stated she'd been worried about me that week, it meant I'd put on a tremendous shitshow the week before.
I never stopped hating Fridays, but I grew less and less afraid of them. Eleanor and I laughed even harder. I told her that occasionally after our sessions, I walked right into Pret and ate a brownie in about five seconds flat, or I went into a shop and bought a ten-quid piece of garbage that I didn't need. She explained that I was worried about what she thought of me, and I agreed. It's not natural to sit in a little room with someone who is detached from the rest of your life and give them all your raw, unedited stories - the ones you've never stated aloud before, the ones you've never told anyone, perhaps not even yourself. But the healthier I became, the less judgement I held for her. In front of me, her true form began to take shape: a woman on my side.
When a friend informed me that it is the relationship between the patient and the therapist, not the talking, that produces healing, I understood. My gradual sensation of quiet and contentment felt like something we were co-creating, like a physio who strengthened a muscle. I brought a small bit of her with me and will continue to do so. The work assisted me in developing a new understanding of

myself, one I will never be able to disregard or bury. She referred to it as "the work." And that's how it's always felt. My time with Eleanor was demanding, confronting, and difficult. She wasn't going to let me get away with anything. She forced me to consider my role in everything. I attempted to remember a time when my actions had no repercussions; after particularly rough Friday afternoons, I wondered what life would have been like if I hadn't opted to go on this journey myself. Would it have been simpler to continue being a drunk jackass in a taxi driving down the M1 at four a.m.? A person whose behaviour was never investigated, but was just ignored, only to reoccur the next weekend?

Eleanor was always telling me that life is a shitshow. Every week, she told me. She warned me that it will let me down. She reminded me that there was nothing I could do to change the situation. I accepted that it was unavoidable.

As we approached our one-year anniversary, our chats became more familiar and relaxed; she selected novels she thought I would enjoy. She generally said 'Goodbye' rather than 'Take care'. When I told her a story, she stopped saying 'Oh no' in a concerned tone, and I started hearing a genuine ecstatic 'Well, this all sounds GREAT!' on a daily basis. I truly ran out of things to tell her one Friday.

I wasn't sure how long I wanted to stay or how liberated I wanted to feel. But I knew that the more I stayed, the more things fell into place. Just as she had anticipated, I talked myself into some peace. I connected the dots and observed the patterns. The conversation began to connect with the action. The gap between how I felt on the inside and how I acted shrank. When things went wrong, I learned to dwell with them, to go deeply, uncomfortably inside instead of venturing to the Outer Hebrides of Experience. The drinking became less frequent, and when it did occur, it was done for celebration rather than escape, so the effect was never terrible.

I felt stronger and more stable. I unlocked the doors within me one by one, emptied the chambers of all my stuff, and talked her through every piece of old toot I discovered inside, before throwing everything out. I knew I was getting closer with each room I opened. A sense of self, a sense of peace. And a sense of belonging.

CHAPTER 10
HEARTBREAK HOTEL

I awoke to three missed Farly calls before seven a.m., as well as a message begging me to call her. She was calling again before I could call her phone. I could tell it wasn't good. I reflected on the last eighteen months since Florence's death, and how Farly had distanced herself from all of her closest friends, burying her sadness in the distance. How I had attempted to entice her back to me, to know what to say to calm her down. When we'd laugh about something and I'd see a flash of her old self, the laughter would change to deep tears and she'd apologise for not understanding how her complete mind or body was operating any longer. I had only one thought: I don't know how I'm going to get her through this again. I took a deep breath and dialled the number.
'Dolly?'
'What's going on?'
'No one has died,' she answered, noticing my fear in my voice.
'OK.'
'This is Scott. 'I suppose we're splitting up.'
It was only eight weeks until their wedding. Farly was alone in their apartment when I arrived an hour later; Scott had gone to work, and her manager had granted her a few days' compassionate leave. She took me through their chat the night before, moment by moment. She informed me that she hadn't expected this, that the wedding was the least of her concerns right now, and that she would do anything to maintain her relationship. Her father and stepmother were spending the weekend at their home in Cornwall, so we decided to travel down there so she and Scott could have some alone time to ponder. We devised a strategy for what she wanted to say to him over the phone. When he called, she requested if I could sit in the same room as her since she was a nervous wreck and needed me in her eyeline to steady herself. As she paced about their flat on the phone, I sat on their sofa and looked around at the home they shared; the life they'd built together. There was a photo of them in their early and mid-twenties, holding each other lovingly; a snapshot of them on their final vacation with Florence. The burnt-orange rug I helped them choose; the sofa on which the three of us sat drinking red wine until

dawn while watching election results on TV. We hung the Morrissey print we bought for their engagement on the wall. I had an unusual and difficult thinking. This was all I had desired for so long. I used to hope that one of them would move on from the other, that we'd always reminisce fondly about Scott the First Love, and that I'd regain my best friend. But now that moment had arrived, and all I could feel was wrenching pain and love for her. They'd been through so much together, and I desperately wanted them to succeed. We had all imagined Farley and Scott's approaching wedding as a kind of Polyfilla over the void left in their family. Whenever her family or any of our friends discussed what the day would be like, we all agreed it would be full of both immense soaring elation and unavoidable pain - but it would undoubtedly signal the beginning of a new chapter in their life. A beginning rather than a conclusion. After Florence's death, I assumed the role of her maid of honour as if it were a knighthood. AJ, Lacey, and I planned a hen party on the same size as the Olympic Opening Ceremony. After months of begging and haggling, an East London hotel handed us their top-floor event space with a view of the city at a heavily discounted fee to host a large dinner. I hired the London Gay Men's Chorus to perform a surprise set of wedding-related songs for Farly while wearing T-shirts with her face printed on them. With the help of a mixologist, I created The Fairly cocktail. I purchased a life-size cardboard cut-out man from eBay and attached a photo of Scott's face to it so that others could snap photos with him. I taped dozens of video messages from individuals wishing her well in her marriage to play like a This Is Your Life VT on the night. Dean Gaffney from EastEnders, two Made in Chelsea cast members, the boy she lost her virginity to, and the boss of her local dry cleaners were among them.
I returned my attention to the chat she was having with Scott.
'Perhaps the wedding became too large,' she speculated. 'You know what I mean? Maybe we let the wedding get out of hand. Maybe we should simply forget about it all and concentrate on ourselves.'
At that precise moment, I received an email from Farly's local MP's office.
To Dolly,
Thank you very much for your email. Andy would be pleased to assist; it appears that you are going above and beyond to ensure that

your buddy has a memorable hen do! Would you be available to shoot at Andy's constituency office next Monday at 11.30 a.m.?
If that isn't possible, I'll check through his journal for another date.
Best regards,
Kristin

I silently removed it.

We drove up to my flat, I tossed a few things in a bag, and texted India and Belle to let them know Farly had tonsillitis and Scott was away on business, so I'd be staying with her for a few days. I felt awful about lying, but since everything was still up in the air and no final decision had been made, I figured it was best to keep things ambiguous so she wouldn't ask any questions. I put up an out-of-office sign and we drove to Cornwall in her car.

We'd taken this route many times before: M25, M4, M5. For holidays at the house in Cornwall, summer road excursions when we were sixteen and seventeen, and journeys from London to university when we were at Exeter. Farly had a strict rating system for all motorway service stations based on their snack shops, and she enjoyed testing me on her preferred order (Chieveley, Heston, Leigh Delamere).

Strangely, a long vehicle ride felt like just what we needed at the time. Our adolescent connection was housed in her automobile. Farly's driver's licence was our passport to freedom during the years I was anxious to be a grown-up. It was our first shared flat, our haven from the outside world. On a hill in Stanmore, there was a vista that looked out over the shining metropolis as if it were Oz. After school, we'd travel there and share a package of Silk Cut and a tub of Ben & Jerry's while listening to Magic FM.

'What do you see when you look at that?' she said a few weeks before we graduated.

'I see all the boys I'll fall in love with, the novels I'll write, the flats I'll live in, and the days and nights that lie ahead. 'What do you notice?'

'Something truly terrifying,' she responded.

The five-hour drive felt considerably longer than usual. Perhaps because it wasn't accompanied by chit-chat, radio, or our scratched Joni Mitchell CDs, but a silence that wasn't a silence; I could hear Farly's head noise. We rested her phone on the dashboard, waiting for Scott to call and admit he'd made a terrible mistake. Her eyes would briefly wander down from the road to the screen whenever her phone lit up.

'Check it out for me,' she'd say hastily. It was always another message from one of our friends, wishing her and her tonsillitis well and asking if she wanted soup and magazines brought over.

'For fuck's sake,' she replied, hardly laughing. 'Me and him have spent the last six years continuously texting about the most boring things, and now all I want to hear from him is a heap of texts of support about a phoney illness.'

'At the very least, you know you're loved,' I suggested. There was more agitated stillness.

'What am I going to say to everyone?' she wondered. 'Everyone at the wedding.'

'You don't need to think about that right now,' I added. 'And if that case arises, you won't have to notify anyone. We can handle everything.'

'I don't know how I'd go through this without you,' she admitted. 'Everything will be fine as long as I have you.'

'I'm right here,' I said. 'I'm not going anywhere,' she says. I'll be here forever, mate. And no matter what that area looks like, we'll make it through together.'

As she stared straight ahead into the darkness of the M5, tears streamed down her cheeks.

'I apologise if I ever made you feel second best, Dolly.'

Richard and Annie were waiting for us when we arrived shortly after midnight. I made tea - in the week following Floss's death, I memorised how everyone drank theirs; it was the only useful thing I could do - and we sat on the sofa, talking over all that had been said and all the conceivable possibilities.

Farly and I were sleeping in the same bed, with the lights turned off.

'Do you know what the true tragedy is in all of this?'

'Go ahead,' she said.

'Me and Lauren have now mastered all of the chords and harmonies of "One Day Like This" for the wedding,' says the singer.

'I know, I know. 'I really enjoyed the recording you sent me.'And the string quartet has now confirmed that they can execute the introduction.'

'I understand.'

'It could be a blessing in disguise,' I reasoned. 'I think the song now makes everyone think of X Factor montages.'
'Are you going to make a loss on the hen do?'
'Don't be concerned about any of it,' I added. 'We'll figure it out.' I waited for her next sentence in the darkness while there was stillness.
'Go ahead,' she said. 'I'm 90% sure it's not occurring right now, so you may as well tell me.'
'But will it make you unhappy?'
'No, it will make me happy.'
I informed her about the special weekend we were planning for her. She groaned with each ludicrous detail, like a child deprived of sweets. On my phone, we watched recordings of the Great and the Good of Britain's D-List sending their best wishes.
'I appreciate you planning it,' she said. 'It would have been fantastic. It would have been perfect for me.'
'We'll do it again for you all.'
'I'm not getting married again.'
'You have no idea. Even if you don't, I'll just shift all those plans to a birthday. I'll wish you a happy fortieth.' Years of bed-sharing and fussing about her falling asleep before the end of a movie meant I could tell she was dropping out. 'Wake me up in the middle of the night if you need me,' I said.
'Thank you, Dolls. 'Sometimes I wish we could simply be in a relationship,' she sighed. 'It would make everything easy.'
'Yeah, but you're not my type, Farly,' she says.
She laughed, then cried a few minutes later. I rubbed her back without saying anything. The next several days were spent going for long walks, going over the identical elements of their last conversation over and over again, attempting to figure out where things went wrong. Farly didn't drink my tea, Richard cooked her meals, and we watched TV while she stared into the distance. I had to return to London for work after a few days. Farly returned to the city a few days later, where she and Scott planned to meet at their neighbourhood park, walk, and sort things out. I couldn't concentrate on anything the morning of their meeting, so I watched my phone like a television, hoping for a message from her. I finally decided to phone her after three hours. She picked up before the first ring was complete.

'It's done,' she said quickly. 'Inform everyone that the wedding has been cancelled. I'll contact you later.'

The phone went silent. I called each of our close friends one by one and told them what had happened; one was as surprised as the last. I carefully prepared a message stating that the wedding had been cancelled and sent it to Farly's half of the guest list. And suddenly it was finished. Extinguished with a copy-and-paste email message and a few phone calls. Their story ended that day, in the future. I demolished every complex component of her hen party, which was scheduled to take place in less than a month, and cancelled everything. Everyone I called, who already knew the wedding had been postponed a year owing to a family tragedy, offered nothing but sympathy. On the day of their chat, Farly left the flat and went to live with Annie and Richard at their family home a few miles away. I returned home, my positive bank account depleted and deep into my overdraft of uplifting words.

'It's as if I'm in jail for something I didn't commit,' she explained. 'I feel like my life is someplace over there, and I'm trapped somewhere over here, told I can't go to it. 'I want to go back to my former life.'

'You'll make it. I swear it won't be like this forever.'

'I've been cursed.'

'No,' I replied. 'You have not been cursed. You've had a dreadful, awful, excruciating run of misfortune. You've experienced more darkness in eighteen months than many people have in a lifetime. But you've got so much light ahead of you that you have to hang on to it.'

'Everyone said that after Florence died. I'm not sure I can take much more.'

Farly returned to work right away, thanks to everyone's support, and our friends launched a military operation to keep her distracted. Despite the fact that it was the most time we'd spent together since we were teenagers, I also sent her a postcard every other day so she'd always have something lovely to return home to after a long day at work. Her bridesmaids whisked her away for a weekend of wine and cooking in the countryside for her hen do. I planned a trip to Sardinia for the week of her wedding. In the month following their breakup, we all took turns spending the evenings with her after work; there wasn't a night that went by without at least one of us there. Sometimes we talked about what was going on, and other times we just sat and ate Lebanese takeout while watching trashy TV. On the drive home, whoever visited would send a message to the rest of us, updating us on how she was and asking who was seeing her next. We were a group of keepers, nurses on duty. Our first-aid kit consisted of Maltesers and Gogglebox episodes. It was at this point that I was reminded of the chain of support that keeps a sufferer afloat: the person in the centre of a crisis requires the support of their family and best friends, and those people require the support of their friends, partners, and family. Even those twice removed may need to speak with someone about it. A broken heart requires a community to mend. I drove back to the flat with Fairly and sat in the car while she went through her possessions and had one last conversation with Scott. Their apartment was put up for sale. Farly unpacked everything into her childhood bedroom - this was a place that was more than transitory but less than forever. The first time any of us saw Farly's old self was on an incredibly terrible Sunday when I roped my friends into performing a picture shoot for a phoney dinner party. It was to go with an article I'd written for a broadsheet culture section about the demise of the traditional dinner party, and the editor requested a photo of me 'entertaining guests' in my flat. I had informed him that I didn't have any male friends available that day, and he had reluctantly agreed to an all-female party. However, when the photographer arrived, it appeared that he had received new instructions to ensure that there were guys in the image. Farly, who had been drinking white wine since she arrived at noon, walked door-to-door along my street, hoping to find a receptive male neighbour. Meanwhile, Belle and AJ drove to our neighbourhood pub, entered, tapped a glass to get everyone's attention, and made a somewhat lame statement that they were searching for a handful of males to be photographed in exchange for some slow-roasted lamb and their image in the paper.

'If this seems like something you'd be interested in,' Belle exclaimed, 'then we'll be waiting outside in the red Seat Ibiza.'

A bunch of sweaty and drunken men in their thirties and forties trudged out of the pub and into the car five minutes later. When we were all crammed around the table, clinking glasses and pretending to be old friends, it became evident that one of the gentlemen was far more inebriated than the rest, eating the roast lamb with his hands like a Roman emperor. The photographer was standing on a chair to get all of us into the image in my very small living room when a light went out and one of the men began yelling for more wine. It was a low-level frenzied slapstick caper with people running around and stuff breaking.

'This is a disaster,' I murmured to the females under my breath.

'Oh, I don't think it's a disaster AT ALL,' Farly snorted. 'I was dumped by my seven-year partner a month ago, so this is a piece of cake!' Even the intoxicated monarch stopped masticating when the photographer looked at me for comfort. 'Cheers,' she remarked cheerfully as she raised her glass to all of us. We rapidly learned how to deal with Farly's suicide bomb jokes, which became a familiar, well-worn piece of furniture in our conversations. You couldn't join in the banter because you didn't know where the black comedy ended and cruelty took over, but you couldn't ignore it either. You couldn't help but laugh out loud. We arrived in Sardinia just a few days before Farly's wedding. We arrived late and drove up to the north-west of the island in our uninsured rental car, carefully winding up coastal roads with the same Joni Mitchell album in the stereo that we'd listened to on our first road trip ten years previously. A time when a relationship seemed ridiculously unattainable, let alone a wedding cancellation. We slept at a simple hotel with a pool, a bar, and a room with a view of the sea - it was all we needed. Farly, the girl who loved school and went on to become a teacher, is and has always been a creature of routine, and we quickly formed our own. We got up early every morning and went directly to the beach to perform some exercise in the dazzling, white light of the early-morning sun before swimming in the sea before breakfast. So I'd go swimming. Farly would sit on the beach and observe. Farly and I disagree on the matter of outdoor swimming; I strip off at the sight of practically any body of open water for a dip, whereas Farly is a chlorinated-pool-only person.

'Let's go!' One morning, when the sea was as calm and pleasant as bathwater, I yelled at the shore. 'You have to come in!' It's really wonderful.'

'But what if there are fish?' she asked, grimacing.

'There are no fish!' I yelled. 'OK, there might be some fish.'

'You know I'm afraid of fish,' she replied.

'You consume them, so how can you be afraid of them?'

'I don't like the idea of them swimming about beneath my feet.'

'You sound so bloody suburban, Farly,' I exclaimed. 'You don't want to lose out on life because you only shop in malls because you're afraid of rain damaging your blow-dry and swim in pools because you're afraid of fish.'
'We are suburban, Dolly; that is exactly what we are.'
'All right! It's entirely natural! It's God's personal swimming pool! It's therapeutic! 'God lives in the sea!'
'If there's one thing I know for certain, Doll,' she rose up and wiped the sand from her legs, 'it's that there is no God!' She exclaimed it excitedly as she paddled into the sea.
We'd spend the morning reading and listening to music before having our first drink of the day around midday. We dozed in the sun all afternoon, then showered and went out for dinner in town to work on our tans. We'd return to the hotel, sip Amaretto Sours on the patio in the heavy blanket of evening heat, play cards, and send tipsy postcards to our friends.
Farly was awake before I was on the wedding day. She fixed her gaze on the ceiling.
'Are you alright?' As soon as my eyes opened, I asked.
'Yeah,' she murmured as she turned away and pulled up the blanket. 'All I want is for today to be over.'
'Today will be one of the most difficult days,' I predicted. 'And then it will be completed. It's over at midnight. You won't have to go through it again.'
'Yeah,' she admitted gently. I sat at the foot of her bed.
'What are your plans for today?' I inquired. 'I've reserved a table at a restaurant with fantastic five-star Trip Advisor ratings that feature awful close-up images of the food like it's a crime scene.'
'That sounds fine,' she sighed. 'I guess I just want to lie on a sun lounger like a normal girl,' she says.
We spent the majority of the day in silence, reading our books and listening to podcasts together with earplugs. She'd glance around and say things like, 'I'd be having breakfast with my bridesmaids right now,' or 'I'd probably be putting on my wedding gown right now.'
She checked the clock on her phone in the middle of the afternoon.
'In England, it's ten to four. I would have been married in exactly ten minutes.'
'Yeah, but at least you're sunbathing in gorgeous Italy instead of floating down a lake with your father in wet Oxfordshire.'

'I was never going to arrive on a gondola,' she exasperatedly admitted. 'I only mentioned it as a possibility because the venue indicated some of the other brides had done it.'
'You did think about it, though.'
'No, I didn't,' she says.
'Yes, you did because I could tell by the tone of your voice that you were waiting for me to say you thought it was a good idea.'
'Not at all!'
'It would have been so awful, everyone watching you as you floated down a lake in a huge dress, then someone throwing you out, the sailor clattering around with the oars.'
'There wasn't a sailor,' she sighed. 'It also lacked oars.'
I went to the bar and ordered a Prosecco bottle.
'Right,' I said, pouring the ice-cold fizz into plastic flutes by the pool. 'You'd be making vows right now. 'I believe we should make vows.'
'To who?'
'To ourselves,' I explained. 'And to one another.'
'OK,' she murmured as she placed her sunglasses on top of her head. 'You get to go first.'
'I promise not to pass judgement on how you handle this when we get home,' I replied. 'It's good to have a really heavy amphetamine and casual sex phase. It's fine if you lock yourself in your house for a year. Whatever you do, you have my support because I can't imagine what it must be like to lose the individuals you've lost.'
'Thank you,' she remarked, sipping her Prosecco and pausing to reflect. 'I promise to always give you room to grow. I'll never tell you that I know who you are since we've known each other since we were children. I know you're going through a lot, and I'll only ever encourage you.'
'That's a good one,' I remarked as I clinked her glass. 'OK, I swear I'll always tell you when you've got something in your teeth.'
'Of course.'
'Especially as we get older and our gums recede. That's when the leafy greens might become extremely stuck.'
'Don't make me feel any worse than I already am,' she pleaded.
'Make a promise to yourself.'
'If I fall in love again, I swear I will never lose sight of my friends,' she remarked. 'I'll never forget how valuable you all are and how much we rely on one another.'

On the night of Farly's wedding reception for over 200 people, we took a taxi up to a hilltop restaurant with a view of the sea.

'You'd be giving your speech right now,' she added. 'Did you ever complete it?'

'No,' I replied. Whenever I've been angry or agitated, I've jotted down some ideas in my iPhone notes. But I haven't finished writing it up yet.'

'I wonder if I would have been joyful for the entire day or if any of it would have been difficult.'

I remembered an article I read on premature death after Florence died, in which an agony aunt encouraged a mourning father not to imagine the life his teenage son might have led if he hadn't been killed in a vehicle accident. She described her fantasy as an exercise in torment rather than comfort.

'You know, that life isn't happening somewhere else,' I explained. 'It does not exist in another world. Your relationship with him lasted seven years. That's all there was to it.'

'I know.'

'Your life has arrived. You're not going to live a tracing-paper version of it.'

'I believe it's better not to think about what could have been.'

'Do not consider it Sliding Doors.'

'I adore that movie.'

'And thank God it's not because no one could ever pull off Gwyneth Paltrow's blonde hair in it.'

Farly replied bluntly, signalling for another carafe of wine, "I'd look like Myra Hindley." 'Did you have any reservations about me and him?'

'Do you want to know the truth?'

'I truly do,' she replied. 'It doesn't really matter now, yet I'd like to know.'

'Yes,' I replied. 'I began to actually love him, and at the end, I believed there was a future where you might be extremely happy. But, certainly, I had reservations.'

She stared out at the setting sun, which sat on the deep-blue Mediterranean horizon like a beautiful peach balanced on a ledge.

'I appreciate you never telling me.'

The sea swallowed the sun, and the sky gradually faded to dusky blue, then night, as if controlled by a dimmer. It was never as horrible as that day again.

We drove down to another coastal town after a week together to meet Sabrina and Belle. The vacation proceeded in the same vein: we drank Aperol, played cards, and lazed on the beach. Belle and I left the apartment around six a.m. one morning, stripped naked on the beach, and swam naked in the sunlight. Farly had both good and bad days during our final week, which was to be expected. We all talked a lot about what had happened, which was the real reason for the holiday. But she also began talking about the future rather than the past, about where she was going to live and what her new routine would be like. It felt like she shed one of her sad skins over the span of a fortnight. One night, she got so drunk - more drunk than we'd been since we were teenagers - that she started hitting on the manager of a local restaurant who looked like a sixty-something Italian John Candy; without a doubt, the most recognizable rite of passage and one that indicates you're in a new phase of getting over a break-up.

Things felt considerably different when we returned to London. Her 29th birthday marked three months since I awoke to three missed calls that morning. It felt like a milestone, so we celebrated properly, going to one of our favourite pubs for dinner and then dancing. She was dressed in the gown I'd found her for the hen party that never happened. It was black, short on either side, and displayed a tattoo she got when she was nineteen, a disastrous, impulsive mistake at a Watford parlour. Two little stars, one pink and the other an ill-conceived yellow ('A Jew with a yellow star tattooed on her!' 'I beg you!' her mother bemoaned).

On the afternoon of her birthday, she went to another tattoo shop to remedy her error from a decade ago. She had the stars filled in with dark ink; she painted it black. She put a 'F' next to one of them for Florence and a 'D' for me. A reminder that no matter what we lose, no matter how uncertain and unpredictable life gets, some people really do walk alongside you forever.

CHAPTER 11
I GOT GURUED

I was requested to write a first piece for a magazine about the hazards of people-pleasing early in Farly's heartbreak summer. The editor I was working for suggested I talk to a man who had just published a new book on the subject. David, a fifty-year-old actor turned writer, was his name. Before we chatted on the phone, I looked him up on Google and noted he had olive skin, salt-and-pepper hair, and kind brown eyes. His publisher emailed me a PDF copy of the book, which was a painfully excellent read. His studies centred on the human urge for validation and how it shortens happiness. Reading it felt like something - or someone - had gripped my shoulders with strong, trustworthy hands and given me a good, sharp, much-needed shaking. We exchanged emails for a bit before scheduling a phone call. His voice was deep and smooth, but much more prominent and theatrical than I had anticipated. His overall aura was that of an outright hippie, but he spoke like an RSC ensemble member. I asked him about the book and the aspects that had particularly resonated with me, and he reminded me that we are continually encouraged as children to control our behaviour. He noted how being instructed not to be bossy, not to show off, or not to be a clever-clogs creates barriers around certain aspects of our personalities that we are afraid to explore as adults. Instead, we hide the aspects of ourselves that are dark, loud, odd, or twisted for fear of being disliked. He contended that it was those aspects of ourselves that were the most beautiful. Because the poem was written from a personal perspective, we had to discuss my own experiences. I informed him that I had begun seeing a therapist earlier this year.
'The danger of someone like you doing therapy is that you appear intelligent,' he remarked. 'You will quickly grasp the theory of it all. In discussion, you'll be able to be academic about yourself. But, you know, all that talking will only get you so far. That change must be felt deeply within you. It can't just be things you talk about with your therapist. 'You need to feel it in your body,' he said slowly, 'in the backs of your knees, in your womb, in your toes, in your fingertips.'
'Hmm,' I murmured, agreeing. We talked for around 45 minutes, ranging from book passages to his years of research and effort, as

well as my own experiences. He addressed me frankly, without any niceties or courtesy. He seems to have gotten directly to my inner equator with just a phone call. He said, 'Pinch that little cheek of yours,' as if he'd known me for years. 'You don't need somebody to tell you what to do or who you should be. You've become your own mother. You must pay attention to what you desire.'
'Hmm,' I managed once more.
'And I want you to take that work seriously every day for the rest of your life.'
'How about being appropriate? 'How does it work when you're always being yourself?'
'Have you ever fallen in love with a man simply because he is suitable?'
'No, not at all.'
'Oooh, that Greg,' he muttered lustfully. 'He's so fucking suitable, he turns me on.'
'No, no, no,' I laughed.
'I'm not concerned with properly. Darkness, edges, and corners are where buried riches can be found. 'Not proper.'
I had the impression he was flirting with me, but I couldn't tell if he was chatting to me so intimately just to get good quotations for the essay. By the end of our talk, we had devolved into a general conversation that didn't feel like an interview at all. I could see he wanted me to tell him if I was in a relationship, but I kept it vague. He mentioned that he thought I could benefit from a one-on-one session with him. 'If you feel comfortable showing all of yourself to someone without fear of being criticised,' he says, 'your closeness will skyrocket.'
'Yeah, that's always been a significant issue for me,' I admitted. 'Intimacy.'

'I know, I can sense it in you.' There was a little pause between us. Maybe he was spewing guru nonsense; maybe what I'd always pushed down was a lot more evident than I realised.
'Hmm,' I managed another time.
'I hope you have someone who truly cares about you, Dolly.'
'I see a therapist,' I explained.
'That wasn't what I meant,' he clarified.

I walked out of my apartment and blinked into the brightness like if I had just awoken.

'I just had the most incredible discussion,' I told India and Belle, who were sunbathing in our garden.

'With whom?' India inquired, removing her earphones.

'That article person - that guru guy.'

'What exactly did he say?'

'I don't know, it was as if he was speaking to something inside me that had never been spoken to before; as if something was yawning and waking up for the first time.'

'That's what they do, isn't it, make you think that's the power they have,' India replied glumly, turning to face the camera. 'I'd never believe somebody who claimed to be a guru.'

'To be fair, he doesn't refer to himself as a guru,' I pointed out.

'Everyone else does,' says the author.

'OK, that's better,' she responded.

'It's a little like being a "maven,"' I went on. 'Or a "mogul" I believe you must wait for someone else to express it. You can't speak for yourself.' I removed my shirt and joined them on the towels they'd spread out on the grass.

'Did he give you what you needed?' Belle inquired.

'Yeah,' I replied. 'He was an excellent interviewee.' I closed my eyes and felt the bright English sunshine hug me. 'I'm not going to be able to quit thinking about Jesus.'

'Like, in a sexy way?' India inquired.

'No, I don't believe so. In an I-want-to-eat-your-soul kind of way. I really want to learn everything I can about him and hear what he has to say.'

'Ask for his phone number,' she said.

'I've already got his phone number. I just spoke with him on the phone.'

'Oh sure,' she replied. 'In that case, just text him.'

'I can't "just text" someone I spoke with for a piece.'

'What's the harm?' Belle inquired.

'Because that would be inappropriate,' I answered, gathering my breath. 'However, who fell in love with it?'

When I went to bed that night, I listened to the recording again, his words bouncing around in my head like a ping-pong ball. The next morning, I finished the piece, sent it to the editor, and promptly forgot about him. A few months later, I was returning home late after a party when I received a WhatsApp message from David. He said he was on vacation in France and had just returned from a long walk beneath the stars when he suddenly remembered our interview and realised he hadn't seen it anywhere.

'This is certainly my selfishness speaking; when will the piece be published?'

'Not at all narcissistic,' I said. 'I'm sorry, it's been postponed due to a problem. I'll text you when it comes out next month. If you are not in the nation, I can send you a copy.'

'I'll be there by then. 'How are you?' he inquired. 'The last time we spoke, you were on the verge of something.'

'I'm still on the verge of something,' I wrote. 'I'm still attempting to transition into a new paradigm. Easy-peasy. 'How are you doing?'

'Same.'

He informed me he had recently ended a long-term relationship. He claimed that an amicable and mutual breakup was the proper thing to do. He informed me that sometimes a break-up is nothing but a relief for both sides, like turning off an air conditioner, the low, constant hum of which you hadn't known was there until everything went silent.

We texted for hours that night, getting to know each other in ways we hadn't gotten from our first talk. We both grew up in North London and attended orthodox boarding schools, which explains why he had a voice that I believed he despised as much as I despised mine. He had four children, two boys and two girls, and he clearly adored all of them. I could detect a dad using his kids as a hookup line a mile away, but this was not one of them. He knew every little detail about each child's personality, passions, dreams, and everyday life, and he talked about them all with genuine interest and devotion.

We discussed music and song lyrics. I told him that my favourite artist was John Martyn, and that his music had been the only love affair I'd had that lasted more than a few years. He told me how he got one of John Martyn's guitars from his ex-wife and offered it to me because he could tell how obsessed I was with his music. We discussed a book we'd both read that had converted me to vegetarianism; we both became enraged at the same statistics and passages. We chatted about our childhood vacations in France. We discussed our parents. We discussed the rain. I told him I loved it even more than blue skies and sunshine. I told him how the rain had always cradled and soothed me, how as a child I would beg my mother if I might sit in the boot of her parked car when it rained. When I read in Rod Stewart's autobiography that he would stand in the middle of the street with his arms outstretched when it rained once a year in LA because he missed it so much, I decided I could never leave England. At three a.m., we said our goodnights.

I awoke the next morning feeling as if I were recovering from a vivid dream. But, sure enough, a new note from David was waiting for me under my pillow, like a dazzling, shining pound coin from the tooth fairy.

'You woke me up around five o'clock this morning,' it said.

'What exactly do you mean?' I responded. He emailed me a recording of the sound of hard and soft rain against his bedroom window.

'Am I the rain?' I inquired, suspending my well-worn pessimism in a manner that would become a regular feature of our conversations.

'You are,' he responded. 'I sensed you getting closer.'

I had to inform my pals about David because I never returned his phone call. We texted each other from the moment we woke up until we went to bed. I set aside roughly five hours a day for working, eating, and washing, but even during those restricted periods, I was thinking about him. I had lunch with Sabrina, and she said she could tell I was staring at my phone screen the entire time.

'All right, enough with the phone,' she declared.

'I'm not looking at my phone!' I responded defensively.

'You're not on your phone, but I can tell you're thinking about talking to him.'

'I'm not,' she says.

'You are, it's like I've taken my thirteen-year-old daughter out to lunch and she wants to go back to MSN Messenger and talk to her foreign exchange student lover.'

'I'm sorry,' I apologised. 'I guarantee I'm not thinking about him.' My phone began to glow.

'What is he sending there?' Sabrina inquired, her gaze fixed on the screen. I showed her a photo of an intricate lion illustration.

'He feels my inner energy is a lion,' she says.

Sabrina gave me a couple puzzled looks.

'Yeah, I don't think your new partner and I will have anything in common,' she stated bluntly.

'No, you will, you will, you will. He's not a solemn, humourless guru; he's quite amusing.'

'All right, just stop texting,' she urged. 'Please. For your benefit. You're going to sabotage your relationship before it even begins. It's almost as if he's a human Tamagotchi.'

'But he'll be in France for three weeks,' I explained. 'I'm not going to stop talking to him until he returns and we can meet.'

'Oh my God, I'm sure he's told you to fly to France, hasn't he?' she said, shaking her head. 'Why are you guys always so extreme?'

'Come on, I'm not going to go,' she says. I said. I didn't tell her I was looking at flights out of curiosity. My pals felt I was strange for becoming so immediately obsessed with someone I didn't know. But they were also used to it - me finding a new love interest had always felt like a greedy child receiving a Christmas present. I pulled the packing open, became frustrated trying to get it to work, obsessively played with it until it shattered, then threw the broken shards of plastic in the back of a cupboard on Boxing Day. I emailed Farley the original interview recording of me and David. 'Pay attention to this,' I wrote. 'And then you'll understand why I'm so crazy about this guy.' I received an email from her an hour later.

'OK, I see why you're behaving so crazy about this dude,' it read.

We talked on the phone about a week after we started messaging. Everything felt different than the last time we met months earlier because the dynamic between interviewer and interviewee had shifted. I could hear his breathing and the crickets in the French countryside late at night. I closed my eyes and could almost feel him next to me; the odd intimacy we'd developed in the previous week.

'It's nice that we're getting to know one other this way before we meet,' he remarked. 'Shelley Winters advised, "Whenever you want to marry someone, go have lunch with his ex-wife."'

'Do you want me to eat lunch with your ex-wife before I eat lunch with you?'

'No, I just think on a first date, people offer such an edited sales presentation of themselves that you don't really get to see much of who that person truly is.'

'Yes, I suppose a sales pitch will be too late by the time we meet.'

Another week has passed, with thousands of texts and dozens of phone calls. I got increasingly interested in him and wanted to know his thoughts on everything. There was no omission; I was lured by

our hair-splitting conversation. He had something new to say about anything I was interested in. Having the light of this man's interest shine on me rejuvenated and renewed me. There simply weren't enough hours in the day to speak with David. I was in desperate need of more, more, more. Texts and phone calls were soon insufficient. We exchanged all of our work. He sent me unpublished chapters of his new book, and I sent him articles and screenplay drafts. We told each other things we wouldn't know if we didn't communicate and look up photographs - that my nails were always bitten down due to my worried nature, and that his fingertips were rough from playing guitar. I watched short films in which he had appeared with rapt attention; I believed he was a genius and told him so, writing down phrases that lingered with me and shots that I adored and called him later to discuss them. 'Go look at the moon,' he suggested late one night while we were on the phone. I put on my trainers and threw my coat over my T-shirt and underwear. I made my way to the end of my street and into Hampstead Heath. He told me about a wild-haired woman he once dated who lived in Highgate and gave him a thirty-second run into the Heath at night before chasing him down. They'd had intercourse in the woods, right next to an oak tree. I sat on a seat overlooking the city skyline, stretched my bare legs beneath the moonlight, and told him about another bench I'd seen here that had made me cry when I read the homage carved into it. It was in the meadow next to the Ladies' Pond, where I swam all summer in honour of Wynn Cornwell, a woman who swam there until she was ninety.'"In memory of Wynn Cornwell, who swam here for more than fifty years, and Vic Cornwell, who waited for her," it says." He must have stood at the gate every day as she swam. Isn't that lovely?'
'You know...' he started to say.
'What?'
'Nothing,' he replied.
'No, go ahead and tell me.'
'You're such a fascinating young lady. In so many ways, you're this open book. 'Why do you do this petulant "I'm an island" nonsense?' he inquired.
'I'm not aware of it; it's not a conscious affectation.'
'You may not believe you can have it, but you can. If you desire it, you can have everything.'

'I can be moved by something and not be sure if I want it for myself,' I explained. 'And I'm simply a sap in the first place. Every year, it's as if a cleaner comes in to vacuum the route between my heart and my tear ducts. One day, it will be simply one big clean stream of filthy, pouring emotions, and by the time I'm your age, I'll probably cry at the sight of a leaf in the breeze.'
'If you're fortunate.'
'Sometimes the disparity between your meagre faith and the unshakeable faith of others is really affecting.'
'I'm not sure. 'Perhaps you just have an unfillable void,' he sighed gently. 'Perhaps no one will ever be able to fill it.' I stared up at the same side of the moon that we were both looking at, wishing on a star that I would go to bed that night and forget what he had said.
'Pay attention to this,' I wrote. 'And then you'll understand why I'm so crazy about this guy.' I received an email from her an hour later.
'OK, I see why you're behaving so crazy about this dude,' it read.
We talked on the phone about a week after we started messaging. Everything felt different than the last time we met months earlier because the dynamic between interviewer and interviewee had shifted. I could hear his breathing and the crickets in the French countryside late at night. I closed my eyes and could almost feel him next to me; the odd intimacy we'd developed in the previous week.
'It's nice that we're getting to know one other this way before we meet,' he remarked. 'Shelley Winters advised, "Whenever you want to marry someone, go have lunch with his ex-wife."
'Do you want me to eat lunch with your ex-wife before I eat lunch with you?'
'No, I just think on a first date, people offer such an edited sales presentation of themselves that you don't really get to see much of who that person truly is.'
'Yes, I suppose a sales pitch will be too late by the time we meet.'
Another week has passed, with thousands of texts and dozens of phone calls. I got increasingly interested in him and wanted to know his thoughts on everything. There was no omission; I was lured by our hair-splitting conversation. He had something new to say about anything I was interested in. Having the light of this man's interest shine on me rejuvenated and renewed me. There simply weren't enough hours in the day to speak with David. I was in desperate need of more, more, more.

Texts and phone calls were soon insufficient. We exchanged all of our work. He sent me unpublished chapters of his new book, and I sent him articles and screenplay drafts. We told each other things we wouldn't know if we didn't communicate and look up photographs - that my nails were always bitten down due to my worried nature, and that his fingertips were rough from playing guitar. I watched short films in which he had appeared with rapt attention; I believed he was a genius and told him so, writing down phrases that lingered with me and shots that I adored and called him later to discuss them.

'Go look at the moon,' he suggested late one night while we were on the phone. I put on my trainers and threw my coat over my T-shirt and underwear. I made my way to the end of my street and into Hampstead Heath. He told me about a wild-haired woman he once dated who lived in Highgate and gave him a thirty-second run into the Heath at night before chasing him down. They'd had intercourse in the woods, right next to an oak tree. I sat on a seat overlooking the city skyline, stretched my bare legs beneath the moonlight, and told him about another bench I'd seen here that had made me cry when I read the homage carved into it. It was in the meadow next to the Ladies' Pond, where I swam all summer in honour of Wynn Cornwell, a woman who swam there until she was ninety.'"In memory of Wynn Cornwell, who swam here for more than fifty years, and Vic Cornwell, who waited for her," it says." He must have stood at the gate every day as she swam. Isn't that lovely?'

'You know...' he started to say.

'What?'

'Nothing,' he replied.

'No, go ahead and tell me.'

'You're such a fascinating young lady. In so many ways, you're this open book. 'Why do you do this petulant "I'm an island" nonsense?' he inquired.

'I'm not aware of it; it's not a conscious affectation.'

'You may not believe you can have it, but you can. If you desire it, you can have everything.'

'I can be moved by something and not be sure if I want it for myself,' I explained. 'And I'm simply a sap in the first place. Every year, it's as if a cleaner comes in to vacuum the route between my heart and my tear ducts. One day, it will be simply one big clean stream of

filthy, pouring emotions, and by the time I'm your age, I'll probably cry at the sight of a leaf in the breeze.'
'If you're fortunate.'
'Sometimes the disparity between your meagre faith and the unshakeable faith of others is really affecting.'
'I'm not sure. 'Perhaps you just have an unfillable void,' he sighed gently. 'Perhaps no one will ever be able to fill it.' I stared up at the same side of the moon that we were both looking at, wishing on a star that I would go to bed that night and forget what he had said. The hours that followed went just as I had predicted. We drank, spoke, listened to music, and kissed while lying close to each other. I inhaled his nude, tattooed skin, which was walnut-brown and dusty from the French sun, as well as the fragrance of tobacco and earth. I focused on the details that a phone and a photograph couldn't capture: the curve of his eyelashes, the way an's slid past his mouth. He paid special attention to me and spoke directly to me; I was open and trusting, and I marvelled at my capacity to experience such intimacy with someone I barely knew.
'Do you know what's funny?' he asked as he kissed my head.
'What?'
'You're just what I expected. Like the playground youngster who covers her eyes with her hands and believes no one can see her.'
'What exactly do you mean?'
'You can't run away from me,' he murmured. I knew this was someone I would never be able to deceive. I knew I was screwed.
'Are you upset that we didn't go on the perfect date first?' As I drifted into the dreamy, murmuring barren region between consciousness and sleep, I inquired.
'No,' he replied as he stroked my hair. 'No, not at all. 'What are your plans for tomorrow?'
'I'm meeting with an editor at one,' I explained.
'Could I come see you later?' he said.
I closed my eyes and was asleep in an instant.
A sound woke me up a few hours later. David was getting ready at the foot of my bed.
'Are you all right?' I inquired, sleepily.
'I'm OK,' he retorted.
'What are your plans?'
'For a spin.'

I looked at the time: 5 a.m.
'Now what?'
'Yes, I'd like to go for a drive.'
'All right,' I said. 'Would you like me to hand over my keys so you can get back in?'
'No,' he replied. He leaned down on the bed and kissed my arm from elbow to shoulder. 'Go back to bed.'
He shut the door. I heard him leave the apartment, get into his car, and drive away. I glanced at my bedroom's white ceiling, attempting to piece together what had happened. I was overcome with a terrible sense of angry rejection. From my stomach to my throat, I felt self-disgust, self-loathing, self-pity, squared. That's how I felt when I got that call from Harry all those years ago.
I crawled into India's bed at seven a.m. and told her everything that had transpired.
'It sounds like he had a nervous breakdown,' India replied.
'How about that?'
'Perhaps it was all too genuine. 'Too close.'
'I mean, the guy's an intimacy coach,' I explained. 'That's his job, literally.'
'Perhaps it's a case of "Those who can, do..."'
'I still can't believe it occurred,' I admitted.
'Whatever his rationale is, he has a fuckload of explaining to do today,' says the author.
'However, he may never talk to me again.'
'Certainly not,' she replied. 'He's a father of four; surely he has more sympathy than that,' says the author.
'If I didn't have the texts on my phone suggesting he was coming over, I'd swear I merely dreamed last night,' I admitted. 'I've been lying awake, torturing myself with these shards of him; his eyes, freckles, and tattoo on his chest -'
'Of course he has a tattoo on his chest,' India remarked, her eyes rolling. 'What exactly is it?'
'I can't. The irony is too much.'
'Go ahead,' she said.
'Something that represents respect for womankind.'
'Jesus sobbed.'
'He should have a footnote added,' I said. 'It has an asterisk next to it. "Apart from Dolly Alderton." '

'Are you all right?' India inquired as she stroked my arm. 'This must have come as a huge surprise.'
'I'm just perplexed,' I explained. 'Is that all?'
David sent me a riddle-like message a couple of hours later.
'Hello,' it said. 'Sorry if that was weird, a bit of an odd exit. It was so nice to see you, touch you - it sent me very deep inside, feeling this abyss between the incredible closeness we've established in the last few days and the reverse, without "knowing" each other.' I sat there watching him type and refusing to respond until I got something that made sense. 'It raised some serious concerns for me. Fuck. I hope you're not in pain; perhaps you're just "Whatever". But maybe you're just odd.' I glanced at my phone, unsure how to answer. 'I hope you didn't wake up depressed this morning,' he wrote. 'I did wake up depressed,' I admitted. 'I don't typically allow people to get close to me.'
'I know. I'm truly sorry. It wasn't an abandoning of you.'
I recalled my last phone call with Harry. How I begged him to love me; how I convinced him through tears that I was good enough for him. How I listened for any tremor in his voice that would lead me to feel I could hold him fiercely, my fingers becoming purple from the grip. That wasn't my tale any longer. That wasn't who I wanted to be.
'I'm not sure what the above implies, but I'm happy to leave it here if it's something you don't feel comfortable continuing,' I wrote.
'I need to pause and clear my thoughts when it comes to you,' he replied. 'I'm not suggesting it should be the end.'
'I am,' I wrote. 'I have to stop now.'
'Shit, I hurt you. 'I can feel it.'
'It's fine,' I said. 'We're both going through weird times in our lives. I'm going through all this analysis because you've just ended a relationship. But I need to defend myself.'
'OK,' he said.
I removed our discussions and call history, and then I deleted David's phone number. As the days passed, I felt a mix of loneliness, shame, grief, and fury. I felt like an idiot, like a frumpy female character on The Archers who is wooed by a devilish, gorgeous stranger before fleeing with all her money. Friends swapped similarly embarrassing experiences to make me feel better, tales of being duped into false intimacy with strangers. One of the editors of my dating column forwarded me an article called 'Virtual Love,' published in a 1997

edition of the New Yorker about the weird new phenomena of falling in love online; a first-person piece from a female journalist who began a phone and email connection with a stranger. 'I may not have known my suitor,' she wrote. 'But, for the first time in my life, I knew the deal: I was a covered person, the target of a blind man's gaze... if we met on the street, we wouldn't know each other, our unique sort of intimacy suddenly shrouded by the branches and bodies and falling debris that made up the physical world.'

Two days after David left me in the middle of the night, the magazine published the article that had first led me to him. I'd completely forgotten about it, but seeing it on the shelves of newsagents felt like everything had gone full circle. I didn't text him to let him know it was out, as I had promised in the initial message that started this disaster. I never spoke to David again.

My pals were stunned by the encounter's aftermath, which grew increasingly ludicrous as time passed. Sometimes, weeks and weeks later, we'd be sitting in the pub, and India would abruptly put down her glass of wine and bark, 'Can you BELIEVE that David guy?' Belle considered reporting him for misusing his position of trust.

'But to whom could you even report him?' I enquired.

'There must be some type of guru council, some sort of Equity thing where they qualify,' India replied.

'Maybe we could just phone Haringey Council,' Belle offered. 'Tell them there is a guru out there who is a risk to naive young women.'

Some said he was just a sexist who saw the challenge of a woman with trust difficulties, got what he wanted, and departed; a wolf in Glastonbury stall-owner's clothing. Others, more gently, thought he was less at ease with the reality of virtual seduction than a millennial. I was used to talking to strangers and building connections with them. Meeting someone in person was always unsettling, but getting to know someone was just the art of narrowing that distance; the 'chasm' he spoke to. That is the fundamental basis of internet dating.

Helen proposed another theory: he was going through a midlife crisis as a result of his break-up, and I was just an impulse buy for his ego. I was a leather jacket or a fast automobile that he enjoyed the notion of but realised after purchasing that it would never work for him or fit into his life. RRHowever, mourning David's death would be like a toddler mourning the loss of an invisible friend. None of it was true. It was speculative; it was fiction. We were sluts for inflated, false sentiment and a desperate yearning to feel something deep within the dark, dank cellar of ourselves. It was just words and blank spaces. It was made of pixels. A game of The Sims; a game of love dress-up. It was doing a tight synchronised dance with satellites.

I only realised who David was after hours of dissection. He wasn't a con artist, a living midlife crisis, or a caddish Don Juan dressed in Birkenstocks and linen. He was the playground kid who covered his eyes and pretended no one could see him. But I could finally see him because we were twins, youngsters as awful as each other. He was disoriented and searching for a lifeboat. He was depressed and needed a distraction. We were two lonely people in desperate need of escapism. He should have known better with twenty years on me, but he didn't. I hope to never be a part of another game like that again. And I'm hoping he finds what he's looking for.

CHAPTER 12
ENOUGH

I made a loud, defensive confession of celibacy in the weeks following my meeting with David, feeling exposed and embarrassed. Of course, it wasn't really celibacy because it only lasted around three months. Second, it was primarily a tactic for attracting male attention; a kind of born-again-virgin fantasy challenge. Which is the polar opposite of what celibacy is supposed to achieve. Because no nun has ever signed a vow of celibacy, she appears to be impossible to seduce. Then there was the calamitous Christmas Special. My buddies developed the term "Christmas Special" to describe a specific form of intoxicated carefree affair that only occurs in the run-up to Christmas; when everyone is high on merriment, goodwill, and advocaat and all bets are off. In the run-up to Christmas, I resolved to acquire a quick fix of validation; a Pot Noodle of self-esteem. After a work party, I emailed a guy I'd been conversing with on a dating app for a couple of weeks, a Geordie with a cheeky smile and good chat-up lines.
'Do you want to go on our date right now?' With an arrogant nonchalance, I messaged him. It was around one o'clock in the morning.
'Sure,' he said.
He arrived at my apartment at two a.m. with a bottle of organic red wine, and we made small conversation on the sofa as if we were two smart metropolitans on an early-evening dinner date, rather than the awful reality of desperation. We began kissing after exactly one hour of conversing. Then we went to my bedroom and had brief, unremarkable sex. It was the physical version of a hurried sandwich in a highway rest stop - something you thought you were looking forward to, only to be disappointed when you got there. Since the night I met Adam in New York, I hadn't had sex with a stranger. I'd grown out of one-night stands by accident, like a small girl who realises one day she no longer wants to play with her Barbies. I knew I didn't want to do it again as soon as it ended. The sex was good, but his presence was intolerable. The illusory closeness of casual sex, which I previously cherished as a student, now seemed like a farcical farce. This was not his fault, but I wanted him out of my flat, out of

my room, out of my bed, which had letters from my friends on the table next to it and a wonderful memory foam mattress topper that I had saved up for. I was uneasy seeing the contour of this stranger's sleeping face in the darkness. The night sluggishly passed.

I awoke with a bad hangover and Geordie was still in my bed. He wanted to spend the morning lying around together, drinking tea and listening to Fleetwood Mac albums - I had a 'boyfriend experience' guy on my hands. The 'boyfriend experience,' I'd noticed over the years, was something certain men offered after a one-night stand in which they behaved inappropriately romantically the next morning to either make you fall in love with them or to alleviate their personal feelings of guilt for having sex with someone whose surname they didn't know. After spooning you and cooking you breakfast, they spent the morning watching Friends episodes before leaving at dusk. They didn't call back. It appeared to be a free service with a concealed high emotional charge. If the 'boyfriend experience' was offered to me, I would never take it.

'Have a wonderful life,' I replied as I stood at the door, having finally gotten him out of my house using a phone launch date.

'Don't say that,' he urged as he hugged me.

'Sorry,' I said, unable to think of anything else to say. 'Merry Christmas,' they say.I sat on the sofa in Leo's old sweater, which I had never thrown away, and watched midday television. India's wonderful lover entered the living room, beard and smile on his face, wearing the warm Fair Isle scarf India had lovingly chosen for him for Christmas. He was a picture of comfort and love, yet I had never felt more distant from him.

'Good morning, Doll,' he said.

'Nice scarf,' she says.

'Yeah, it is, isn't it?' he remarked, smiling down at it. 'India informed me last night that you commissioned a Christmas Special.'

'Yeah,' I murmured, my face half-buried in the sofa cushion, my gaze fixed on the Loose Women panel.

'Good?'

'No. Awful. 'Depressing,' I said. 'It was the Christmas Special of EastEnders.'

'Oh dear,' he exclaimed. 'So there will be no recommissioning?'

'No. It was a one-time occurrence.'

My dating column finally ended the next month, giving me no excuse to continuously be seeking for the next guy under the premise of it being my career. The end of the column could easily have signalled the start of a new phase in my life, one that wasn't governed by late-night phone calls from old boyfriends, right-swiping and left-swiping, cornering men at dinner parties, and coordinating cigarette breaks in the pub when there was an attractive man outside.

The truth was that the column was an enabler, but I was an addict. I had always been, long before I was sexually active. Jilly Cooper reveals on Desert Island Discs that when she was at an all-girls school, she was so infatuated with boys that she fantasised about the eighty-year-old man gardener who would occasionally work in the grounds. Growing up, I was that girl, and in some ways, I never stopped being that girl. Boys captivated and terrified me in equal measure; I didn't understand them and didn't want to. Their purpose was to bring gratification, whilst female friends provided everything else that was important. It was a tactic for keeping boys at bay. When Farly and I returned from Sardinia and she embarked on her new life as a single woman for the first time since her early twenties, I delivered an imperious TED lecture on the intricacies of modern dating.

'The first thing you need to understand is that no one meets in real life anymore,' I remarked. Farly, things have changed since you were last on the market, and you have little choice but to change with them.'

'OK,' she murmured, nodding and mentally collecting notes.

'The good news is that no one enjoys online dating. We're all doing it, but we're all hating it, so we're all in the same boat.'

'Right.'

'However, you must not be offended if you find yourself in a pub or elsewhere and not getting talked to. It's perfectly natural. For instance, a man may enjoy the sight of you at a party but not speak to you, but then Facebook messages you later saying he wishes he had.'

'Weird.'

'Very much so, but you grow used to it. It's just a different method of building that first connection.'

'How about tit-wanks?' she inquired.

'But what about them?'

'Do tit-wanks still exist?'

'No,' I answered emphatically. Since 2009, no one has given or gotten one. It will never be demanded of you.'
'OK, at least that's one good thing,' she said.
A week later, Farly met a guy in a bar. They swapped phone numbers. They started seeing each other right away.
'Farly's met someone,' I told India at breakfast on Saturday morning.
'Well done,' she answered. 'One or two slices of toast?'
'Two. You won't believe where. Guess.'
'I'm not sure,' she admitted as she ate a scoop of lemon curd.
'In a bar,' he says.
'What exactly do you mean by "in a bar"?'
Like, in real life. He approached her and began talking, and they are now dating. Are you kidding me? I'm delighted for her, but I'm also furious. I mean, when was the last time you met someone in a bar?'
'How ludicrous!' India expressed genuine fury.
'I know,' I admitted. 'I know.'
Belle entered the kitchen in her dressing robe.
'Good morning, kittens,' she murmured sleepily.
'Did you hear anything about it?' India inquired angrily. 'How about Farly's new guy?'
'No,' she said.
'They met in a bar,' says the author.
'Which bar?'
'I'm not sure,' I admitted. 'Richmond, I believe. Are you kidding me? I don't think I've given somebody my phone number on a night out in around five years, and it happens to her every five minutes.'
'Perhaps it's a south of the river thing,' Belle speculated.
'I believe it's a fair thing,' I explained. When it comes to love, the differences between Farly and me are never more clear. Farly is a comfortable, cohabiting, dedicated, long-term monogamist. The period of a relationship that I enjoy the most - the unknown, the high-risk, the exciting first few months when you can barely eat because of butterflies in your stomach - is the part she despises. Barbecues at a boyfriend's family home, two cooked potatoes on the sofa in front of the TV on a Saturday night, long car rides on highways together are utter joy for her. She would gladly trade three months of passion for a lifetime of domesticity, companionship, practical goals, and baked potatoes. I'd give anything for a lifetime of repeating those first three months and a guarantee that I'd never have

to go to an Ikea, a National Express coach station, or a relative's house outside of the M25 with a sexual partner.

'Projecting' is one of those therapy terms you pick up along the way. It involves accusing someone else of doing or being exactly what you fear you are in order to avoid responsibility; it's 'watch-the-birdie' blame. When it came to Farly's romantic decisions, I did it a lot. I'd always thought of my constant opposition to commitment as an act of liberation; I hadn't known it was the source of my feeling trapped. Farly may have always felt the need to be in a relationship, but at least she was clear about what she wanted. I needed something but had no idea what it was, and I despised myself for wanting it.

Farley and I went for a long walk, and I told her about my ambitions to take a genuine vacation from sex, with all of its prologues and epilogues of flirting, messaging, dating, and kissing, in order to gain some autonomy. I informed her that, despite being unmarried for the majority of my life, I'd realised I hadn't been truly single since I was a teenager. She concurred and stated that she believed it was a fantastic idea.

'Do you think I'll ever feel settled in a relationship?' As we leaped over logs in Hampstead Heath's woodlands, I questioned her.

'Of course I do,' she says. You simply haven't met the proper man yet.'

'Yes, but here's the catch. I don't believe it's about finding the right man; I believe it's about finding myself. 'I think the men are kind of irrelevant until I figure this out.' I waved at myself, exhausted, as if I were a teenager's dirty bedroom.

'Well, I think it's great that you're putting in the effort. I believe it will be short-term work for long-term gain.'

'How come you find it so simple?' I inquired of her. 'I was always jealous of how easy things were for you with Scott. You just walked in, and boom. Committed.'

'I genuinely don't know.'

'Did you ever assume when you were engaged that you'd never sleep with anybody else? Didn't that bother you?'

'Do you know what,' she continued, 'now that you've said that, I don't think I ever thought about it once.'

'That can't be true,' I exclaimed, bouncing like a child and walking till my fingertips reached a tree branch.

'Honestly, and I know it seems strange, but I don't think the thought ever occurred to me,' she said. 'All I wanted was a future with him,' she says.

'I want to know what it's like to be completely dedicated to someone instead of having one foot out the door.'

'You're too hard on yourself,' she pointed out. 'You are capable of long-term love. You've done it better than anyone I've ever met.'

'How? 'My longest romance lasted two years and ended when I was twenty-four.'

'I'm referring to you and me,' she explained.

I couldn't stop thinking about Farly's remarks for the next few days; I remembered how we'd known each other for twenty years and how I'd never grown tired of her. I reflected on how I'd grown more in love with her as we got older and enjoyed more experiences. I reflected on how happy I am to tell her about good news or to hear her opinion when a crisis occurs; how she is still my favourite person to go dancing with. The more history we shared together, the more valuable she became, like a gorgeous, priceless work of art hanging in my living room. Her love showered me in familiarity, comfort, and a sense of serenity. All this time, I had been made to believe that my worth in a relationship was determined by my sexuality, which is why I always acted like a cartoon nymphomaniac. I never imagined that a man could love me the way my friends do; that I could love a man with the same devotion and care as I love them. Perhaps I had been in a wonderful marriage without even realising it. Perhaps Fairly represented what a good relationship felt like.

I poured myself into abstinence as if it were a PhD project. The more I read about sex and love addiction in books, tales, and blogs, the more I knew where I had gone so wrong. Dating had devolved into a source of immediate fulfilment, an extension of narcissism, and had little to do with connecting with another person. I had often built intensity with a man and mistook it with intimacy. At JFK, a stranger proposed to me. A middle-aged guru invited me to spend a week with him in France. It was exaggerated, unnecessary intensity, and there was no personal connection with another person. Intimacy and intensity. How did I get them so messed up?

After a month, I felt nothing but complete and utter relief. My phone's dating applications were erased. I removed the phone numbers I had booty-called. I stopped responding to ex-boyfriends who would text me at three a.m. with seemingly innocuous questions like 'How's it hangin' m'lady?' Alternatively, 'What's the dealio smith?' I quit stalking possible conquests online and deactivated my Facebook account as a result. I stopped keeping secrets. I came to an end around midnight. I devoted my entire time to my work and my friendships. Two months have gone by. I learned what it was like to attend a wedding and genuinely be present to witness your friends' marriages, rather than treating it like an eight-hour meat market. I discovered what it was like to sit back and enjoy the wonderful, bell-like sound of a choir singing in church, rather than frantically scanning the aisles, checking the fingers of all the males to see which were single. I learned how to enjoy a man's conversation at dinner regardless of his marital status; how to avoid battling for the attention of the lone single man at the table by saying something improper in a faintly threatening tone of Sid James bawdiness. At a gathering, I saw Leo for the first time in five years and met his new wife; I hugged them both and then left them alone. I was not angry when Harry got engaged. I texted Adam to congratulate him on his new relationship. Their stories were no longer relevant to me, and I no longer need their attention. I finally felt like I was jogging down my own road, collecting my own pace and momentum. Rather than trying to grab any man's attention, I sat on tubes and got lost in my book. Instead of feverishly doing circuits of the room till the very end in the hope of finding someone I liked, I left parties when I chose to leave them. I didn't attend gatherings just because I knew certain people would be there; I didn't plan chance meetings with people I liked. I went out dancing with Lauren one night, and instead of trying to find a guy of my own, I stayed in the centre of the dance floor for an hour and danced by myself, sweating and swaying and spinning and spinning.

'Are you waiting for someone?' a man inquired, drawing me closer.
'No, she's right here,' I murmured, taking his hands away from me.
'I never thought I'd use this word in regard to you, and I don't want you to take offence,' Fairly stated three beers later in the pub. 'But I've found your company to be really soothing in recent months.'
'Can you remember the last time you saw me calm?' I inquired.
'Well, I just haven't,' she said as she drained the remnants of her vodka tonic and crunched on an ice cube. 'Ever. In over two decades.'

I flew to the Orkney Islands in late April to write a story for a travel magazine on vacation alone. I lived above a tavern overlooking the harbour of Stromness, and after a beer and a steaming bowl of mussels downstairs, I'd go for a long walk along the coast and gaze up at the enormous open heavens - vaster than any sky I'd ever seen.

After a few days of quiet alone with my thoughts, I wandered under the stars and down the cobblestone alleys one night, and an idea crept all over me like captivating, brilliant wisteria blooms. I don't need a dazzlingly charismatic artist to pen a song about me. I don't need a guru to tell me stuff about myself that I'm not aware of. I don't have to take off all my hair because a boy said it would look good on me. I don't need to modify my appearance to be worthy of someone's love. I don't need a man's words, glances, or comments to believe I'm visible; to believe I'm here. I don't need to flee from discomfort and into a male gaze. That isn't where I come to life. Because I am sufficient. My heart is sufficient. The stories and sentences that swirl around in my head are enough. I'm fizzing, bubbling, buzzing, and exploding. I'm boiling over and on fire. My early-morning hikes and late-night baths are sufficient. My raucous laughter at the pub is sufficient. My loud whistle, shower singing, and double-jointed toes are enough. I'm a freshly poured pint with a nice, frothy head. I am my own universe, my own galaxy, my own solar system. I'm the opening act, the main event, and the backup vocalists. And if this is it, if this is all there is - just me, the trees, the sky, and the seas - I know it's enough. I am sufficient. I am sufficient. The words ricocheted through my body, shaking every cell. I felt them, I comprehended them, and they became ingrained in my bones. Like a racehorse, the notion galloped and hopped through my system. I yelled it into the night sky. My statement bounced from star to star, leaping from carbon to carbon like Tarzan. I am entire and whole. I'll never be out.

And I am more than adequate.

(I believe they call it a "breakthrough.")

CHAPTER 13
HOMECOMING

There's a lot about love that I don't understand. First and foremost, I haven't been in a relationship for more than a couple of years. Sometimes I hear married folks describe a 'phase' of their relationship as lasting longer than my longest relationship. This appears to be prevalent. I've heard people refer to the first ten years of their marriage as "the honeymoon phase." My honeymoon stages have been known to last only a few minutes. Friends of mine describe their connection as if it were a third person in their relationship, a living thing that twists and morphs and moves and evolves the longer they're together. An organism that changes as much as two humans do over the course of their lives. I'm not sure what it takes to foster the third being. I'm not sure what true long-term love feels or looks like on the inside. I also have no idea what it's like to live with someone you love. I have no idea what it's like to go house looking with a friend, to scheme against an estate agent in a sneaky whisper from the bathroom. I have no idea what it's like to sleepily choreograph my way around someone in the bathroom every morning as we take turns brushing our teeth and using the shower in a familiar ritual. I have no idea what it's like to know you'll never be able to leave and return home again; that your home is there next to you every morning and night. In truth, I have no idea what it means to work as a team with a partner; I've never relied on a romantic relationship for support or relaxed into its pace. But I've been in love and lost love, and I know what it's like to leave and be abandoned. I'm hoping that one day the rest will follow. Almost all I know about love I've learned from long-term female friendships. Especially those I've lived with at one point or another. I know what it's like to know every little detail about someone and luxuriate in that information as if it were a subject. I'm like the woman who can predict what her spouse would eat at every restaurant when it comes to the girls I've made houses with. I know India doesn't drink tea, AJ prefers cheese and celery sandwiches, pastry gives Belle heartburn, and Fairly prefers her toast cold so the butter spreads but doesn't melt. AJ requires eight hours of sleep to function, Farly seven, Belle six, and India can get by on a Thatcherite four or five. Farly's alarm clock is

'So Far Away' by Carole King, and she enjoys viewing narrative-driven obesity shows like Half-Ton Mom and My Son, The Killer Whale. AJ watches old Home and Away episodes on YouTube and buys sudoku books to do in bed. Belle exercises in her bedroom before going to work and listens to trance music in the bath. India spends her weekends doing jigsaw puzzles in her bedroom and watching Fawlty Towers. ('I just don't know how she gets so much mileage out of it,' Belle once quietly said. 'There are only twelve episodes,' she says.)

I know what it's like to eagerly strap on an oxygen tank and dive deep into a person's idiosyncrasies and flaws, relishing every intriguing moment of discovery. For example, Farly has always slept in a skirt since I've known her. Why does she behave in this manner? So what's the point? Or that Belle tears her flesh-coloured tights off when she gets home from work on Friday nights - is this a sign of her silent wrath against the corporate system, or just a routine she's grown fond of? When AJ feels fatigued, she puts a scarf around her head; this isn't cultural appropriation, then what is it? Was she swaddled too much as a newborn, giving her a calm sense of infantilization? India sleeps with her comfort blanket, a ragged old navy jumper she names Nigh Nigh. Why does she refer to it as 'he'? And when she realised it was a boy, how old was she? In fact, I would love nothing more than to have a literary salon in which all of my cherished friends bring their childhood comfort blankets to the table and we explore their gender identities. That, believe it or not, would be completely fascinating to me.

I know what it's like to set up and run a home with others. I understand what a shared economy of trust is; knowing that someone will always lend you £50 until payday and that once you've paid it back, they may need to borrow the same amount from you ('We're like primary school kids continually swapping sandwiches,' Belle once observed of our salary. 'One week you need my tuna and sweetcorn, the next week I need your egg and cress'). I remember the excitement of getting mail in December and seeing cards with three names inscribed on the front that made you feel like a family. When you enter into online banking and find three surnames on one account, you get a peculiar sense of security.

I understand how it feels to have an identity that is larger than just you; to be a member of a 'us'. I know what it's like to overhear Farly say to someone across the table, 'We don't really eat red meat,' or to hear Lauren say, 'That's our favourite Van Morrison record,' to a boy she's chatting up at a party. That feels surprisingly pleasant to me.

I understand what it's like to go through a traumatic situation and then turn it into common mythology. We do the same with our own micro-disasters as the couple who theatrically tells the story of their bags getting lost on their last vacation, each taking a line. Like when India, Belle, and I relocated and everything that could possibly go wrong did. The reality was misplaced keys, borrowing money from friends, staying on couches, and storing belongings. The narrative is fantastic.

I understand what it's like to love someone and accept that you can't change certain aspects of them; Lauren is a grammatical pedant, Belle is messy, Sabrina's texts are endless, AJ will never reply to me, and Farly is often moody when tired or hungry. And I know how liberating it is to be loved and accepted for all of my shortcomings (I'm usually late, my phone is never charged, I'm oversensitive, I obsess over trivial matters, and I let the trash can overflow).

I know what it's like to hear someone you care about recite a narrative you've heard 5,000 times to an entranced audience. I can imagine that person (Lauren) embellishing it more flamboyantly each time ('it happened at eleven' becomes so this was at four a.m.'; 'I was sitting on a plastic chair' becomes 'and I'm on this sort of chaise longue hand-crafted from glass'). I know what it's like to be so in love with someone that this doesn't bother you at all; to let them sing this well-rehearsed tune and maybe even join in with the supportive high-hat to speed up the story when they need it.

I understand how a relationship crisis feels. When you think: either we address this situation and try to fix it, or we separate. I know what it's like to agree to meet in a South Bank bar, start bristly, and end three hours later, weeping in each other's arms, vowing never to make the same mistakes again (people only meet on the South Bank to reconcile or break up - I've done some of my best dumping and being dumped in the National Theatre bar).

I know what it's like to feel like you've always got a lighthouse - lighthouses - to guide you back to land; to feel the warmth of its beam clasp your hand as it stands next to you at a funeral for someone you care about. Or to follow its flash across a crowded room at a bad party where your ex-boyfriend and his new wife unexpectedly showed up; the flash that screams, Let's get chips and the night bus home.

I understand that love can be raucous and joyous. It can be shouting 'YOU ARE FUCKING AMAZING' above the music while dancing in the swampy muck and pouring rain at a festival. It's introducing them to your coworkers at a work function and taking delight in watching them make people laugh and make you appear lovable simply by being liked by them. It makes you giggle until you cough. It's waking up in a nation none of you has ever visited. It's skinny-dipping time in the morning. It's walking down the street with someone on a Saturday night and having the impression that the entire city is yours. It's a massive, gorgeous, and exuberant force of nature.

And I'm also aware that love is a really quiet thing. It's lying on the sofa drinking coffee and chatting about where you're going to drink more coffee the next morning. It's folding down pages from books you believe they'd like. It's when people forget to take their clothing out of the washing machine and hang it up before leaving the house. 'You're safer here than in a car, and you're more likely to die in one of your Fitness First Body Pump classes than in the next hour,' it says as they hyperventilate on an easyJet flight to Dublin. 'Hope today goes well,' 'How did today go?,' 'Thinking of you today,' and 'Picked up loo roll' are the texts. I know that love happens beneath the glory of the moon, stars, fireworks, and sunsets, but it also happens while you're resting on blow-up air beds in your childhood bedroom, sitting in A&E, in line for a passport, or stuck in traffic. Love is a peaceful, reassuring, relaxing, pottering, pedantic, harmonising hum; something you can easily forget is there, despite the fact that its palms are outstretched beneath you in case you fall.

Before it ended, I had lived with my pals for five years. Farly had left me for her lover, AJ had left, and India had called me one day to say she was ready to do the same, before breaking down in sobs.

'Why are you crying?' I inquired. 'Is this because of how I treated Fairly when she met Scott? Were you worried I'd go insane? Do you all think I'm crazy? That was four years ago; I'm more prepared to handle this today.'

'No, no,' she exclaimed. 'I'm just going to miss you,' she says.

'I know,' I admitted. 'I'm going to miss you as well. But you're turning thirty this year. And it's wonderful that your partnership is ready to take the next step. It's very natural for things to change.' I was taken aback by my own logic and quietly granted myself a CBE for services to friendship.

'What are you planning to do?' she inquired. 'You've always mentioned how much you'd like to live on your own.'

'I'm not sure. 'I'm not sure if I'm prepared,' I admitted. 'Perhaps I should live with Belle until she decides to live with her partner. It gives me at least six months to figure out what I'm going to do next.'

'You're not The Hunger Games, Dolly,' she remarked. 'It shouldn't be an endurance test among our buddies to see who can hang in there the longest.'

I recognized that I had been given a chance. I could wait until all of my friends had met men and moved out. I could rent from strangers on Gumtree who kept shaving cream in the fridge in the hopes that I'd find a boyfriend and leave shortly. Or I could make up my own story.

Finding a one-bedroom flat to rent within my budget wasn't simple; I was taken to a lot of homes that had mattresses next to the stoves and showerheads balanced over a lavatory in a 'wet room'. There was the spacious one-bed of twenty square metres and the one with police tape around the front door. India accompanied me to viewings, bargaining and questioning estate agents' bluster and asking whether I truly believed I could live without a closet and instead kept all my clothing in a suitcase under the bed.

But, eventually, I found an apartment in the heart of Camden that I could just about afford. It was a ground-floor apartment with a bedroom, bathroom, and living area, as well as enough space for a closet and a shower that hung over a bath. At the back, there was a sunken, wet kitchen with no drawers and a porthole window with a canal view that made me feel like I was on a boat. It wasn't flawless, but it was mine.

All of us who had previously lived together went on a 'farewell flat-sharing' pub crawl in our twenty-something haunts. We arrived dressed as a couple in their twenties, which was as insane as it sounds. AJ dressed up as Gordon, our first landlord, complete with a leather biker jacket, white shoes, a short brown wig, and a persistent smarmy grin. Farly arrived as a big Henry vacuum in a spherical costume with a pipe connected that dragged around the ground the more she drank. Belle arrived as our obnoxious nightmare neighbour, complete with smudged lipstick and a Cher wig. India arrived dressed like a large bin, as emptying, relining, or taking one out seemed to be the most common theme of our time together, with bin liners tied around her shoes, a lid for a hat, and empty face-wipe and Monster Munch packets clinging to her body. I came dressed as a large packet of smoke and quickly regretted it when people approached me begging for free cigarettes, figuring I was some sort of Marlboro Lights promotion gal banging the streets of Kentish Town.

We went from pub to pub before returning to our original yellow-brick residence. We even stopped by Ivan's corner shop, only to learn from his coworker that he'd inexplicably "gone abroad for some unfinished business" and vanished "without a trace."

'The artists have gone,' Belle mused as we went down the crescent, day becoming dusk. 'Now the bankers will arrive.'

A week later, I taped up my pot plants and paperbacks in cardboard boxes for my new home. On our last night together, India, Belle, and I drank discounted Prosecco - the tipple of a bloody decade - and drunkenly danced around our empty living room to Paul Simon. We huddled in the corner of our wine-stained carpet the next morning, our knees knocking together as we sat side by side, talking very little while we waited for our different moving vans. I understand that love can be raucous and joyous. It can be shouting 'YOU ARE FUCKING AMAZING' above the music while dancing in the swampy muck and pouring rain at a festival. It's introducing them to your coworkers at a work function and taking delight in watching them make people laugh and make you appear lovable simply by being liked by them. It makes you giggle until you cough. It's waking up in a nation none of you has ever visited. It's skinny-dipping time in the morning. It's walking down the street with someone on a Saturday night and having the impression that the entire city is yours. It's a massive, gorgeous, and exuberant force of nature.

And I'm also aware that love is a really quiet thing. It's lying on the sofa drinking coffee and chatting about where you're going to drink more coffee the next morning. It's folding down pages from books you believe they'd like. It's when people forget to take their clothing out of the washing machine and hang it up before leaving the house.

'You're safer here than in a car, and you're more likely to die in one of your Fitness First Body Pump classes than in the next hour,' it says as they hyperventilate on an easyJet flight to Dublin. 'Hope today goes well,' 'How did today go?,' 'Thinking of you today,' and 'Picked up loo roll' are the texts. I know that love happens beneath the glory of the moon, stars, fireworks, and sunsets, but it also happens while you're resting on blow-up air beds in your childhood bedroom, sitting in A&E, in line for a passport, or stuck in traffic. Love is a peaceful, reassuring, relaxing, pottering, pedantic, harmonising hum; something you can easily forget is there, despite the fact that its palms are outstretched beneath you in case you fall.
Before it ended, I had lived with my pals for five years. Farly had left me for her lover, AJ had left, and India had called me one day to say she was ready to do the same, before breaking down in sobs.
'Why are you crying?' I inquired. 'Is this because of how I treated Fairly when she met Scott? Were you worried I'd go insane? Do you all think I'm crazy? That was four years ago; I'm more prepared to handle this today.'
'No, no,' she exclaimed. 'I'm just going to miss you,' she says.
'I know,' I admitted. 'I'm going to miss you as well. But you're turning thirty this year. And it's wonderful that your partnership is ready to take the next step. It's very natural for things to change.' I was taken aback by my own logic and quietly granted myself a CBE for services to friendship.
'What are you planning to do?' she inquired. 'You've always mentioned how much you'd like to live on your own.'
'I'm not sure. I'm not sure if I'm prepared,' I admitted. 'Perhaps I should live with Belle until she decides to live with her partner. It gives me at least six months to figure out what I'm going to do next.'
'You're not The Hunger Games, Dolly,' she remarked. 'It shouldn't be an endurance test among our buddies to see who can hang in there the longest.'
I recognized that I had been given a chance. I could wait until all of my friends had met men and moved out. I could rent from strangers on Gumtree who kept shaving cream in the fridge in the hopes that I'd find a boyfriend and leave shortly. Or I could make up my own story.
Finding a one-bedroom flat to rent within my budget wasn't simple; I was taken to a lot of homes that had mattresses next to the stoves and

showerheads balanced over a lavatory in a 'wet room'. There was the spacious one-bed of twenty square metres and the one with police tape around the front door. India accompanied me to viewings, bargaining and questioning estate agents' bluster and asking whether I truly believed I could live without a closet and instead kept all my clothing in a suitcase under the bed.

But, eventually, I found an apartment in the heart of Camden that I could just about afford. It was a ground-floor apartment with a bedroom, bathroom, and living area, as well as enough space for a closet and a shower that hung over a bath. At the back, there was a sunken, wet kitchen with no drawers and a porthole window with a canal view that made me feel like I was on a boat. It wasn't flawless, but it was mine.

All of us who had previously lived together went on a 'farewell flat-sharing' pub crawl in our twenty-something haunts. We arrived dressed as a couple in their twenties, which was as insane as it sounds. AJ dressed up as Gordon, our first landlord, complete with a leather biker jacket, white shoes, a short brown wig, and a persistent smarmy grin. Farly arrived as a big Henry vacuum in a spherical costume with a pipe connected that dragged around the ground the more she drank. Belle arrived as our obnoxious nightmare neighbour, complete with smudged lipstick and a Cher wig. India arrived dressed like a large bin, as emptying, relining, or taking one out seemed to be the most common theme of our time together, with bin liners tied around her shoes, a lid for a hat, and empty face-wipe and Monster Munch packets clinging to her body. I came dressed as a large packet of smoke and quickly regretted it when people approached me begging for free cigarettes, figuring I was some sort of Marlboro Lights promotion gal banging the streets of Kentish Town.

We went from pub to pub before returning to our original yellow-brick residence. We even stopped by Ivan's corner shop, only to learn from his coworker that he'd inexplicably "gone abroad for some unfinished business" and vanished "without a trace."

'The artists have gone,' Belle mused as we went down the crescent, day becoming dusk. 'Now the bankers will arrive.'

A week later, I taped up my pot plants and paperbacks in cardboard boxes for my new home. On our last night together, India, Belle, and I drank discounted Prosecco - the tipple of a bloody decade - and drunkenly danced around our empty living room to Paul Simon. We huddled in the corner of our wine-stained carpet the next morning, our knees knocking together as we sat side by side, talking very little while we waited for our different moving vans.

Farly, the most efficient and organised person I've ever met, came over the day I moved into my new house to assist me with unpacking ('Are you sure you want to do this?' I sent her a text message. 'Please, this tastes like cocaine to me,' she said. We ordered Vietnamese cuisine and sat on the floor of my living room, slurping pho and dipping summer rolls in sriracha sauce as we discussed where we should put the sofa, chairs, lamps, shelving, and where I would sit and write every day. We unpacked late into the night before falling asleep on my mattress propped up against the bedroom wall, surrounded by shoe boxes, clothing bags, and book stacks.

Farly had already left for work when I woke up, and there was a letter on the pillow in her plump childlike handwriting that hadn't altered since she put notes on my lever-arch files in Tipp-Ex during science GCSE lectures. 'I adore your new home and you,' it said.

The morning sun rushed into my bedroom and formed a dazzling white puddle on my mattress. In my bed, I spread out diagonally across the soft sheet. I was utterly alone, but I'd never felt more secure. It wasn't the bricks I'd managed to rent or the roof over my head that I was most thankful for. It was the home I now carried like a snail on my back. The feeling that I was finally in capable and caring hands.

In my empty bed, there was love. It had heaped up in the recordings Lauren purchased me as an adolescent. It was in my kitchen cottage, between the pages of cookbooks, on smudged recipe cards from my mother. Love was in the gin bottle tied with a ribbon that India had brought for me; it was in the smeary photo strips with curled corners that would wind up plastered to my fridge. It was in the note on the pillow next to me, the one I'd roll up and store in the shoebox with all the other notes she'd written previously.

I awoke in my one-woman boat, safe and sound. I was floating in a sea of love, gliding into a new vista.

It was right there. Who'd have guessed? It had always been there.

The contents of this book may not be copied, reproduced or transmitted without the express written permission of the author or publisher. Under no circumstances will the publisher or author be responsible or liable for any damages, compensation or monetary loss arising from the information contained in this book, whether directly or indirectly. .

Disclaimer Notice:

Although the author and publisher have made every effort to ensure the accuracy and completeness of the content, they do not, however, make any representations or warranties as to the accuracy, completeness, or reliability of the content. , suitability or availability of the information, products, services or related graphics contained in the book for any purpose. Readers are solely responsible for their use of the information contained in this book

Every effort has been made to make this book possible. If any omission or error has occurred unintentionally, the author and publisher will be happy to acknowledge it in upcoming versions.

Copyright © 2023

All rights reserved.

Printed in Great Britain
by Amazon